THE MEASURE OF LOVE

God's Two Commandments

by

Michael R. Hodge
with Amanda Hodge

THE MEASURE OF LOVE

By Michael R. Hodge
with Amanda Hodge

Italics and/or bold in Scripture quotations are the author's emphasis.

Printed in the United States of America

First Edition: 2006
Second Edition: March 2011

Hodge, Michael R.
The measure of love : God's ten commandments for your daily life / Michael R. Hodge. – 2nd ed.

ISBN 978-1-257-12184-7

CONTENTS

PAGE

Acknowledgements

Although my name appears on the cover of this book, there are many who participated in this project. This book originally was created within the context of a sermon/devotional series that was developed while I was serving as an Associate Pastor. Our pastor brought the weekly messages and I wrote the accompanying devotionals to prepare our congregation for the message the following Sunday. Now, five years later, this book has been revised and updated in order to now accompany my own sermon series on the Ten Commandments. As this book finds a new audience within a new congregation the purpose remains the same – to lead the reader to understand the measure of God's love discovered within the Ten Commandments.

Producing weekly devotionals with material for five days of the following week was quite a task several years ago. There were those that proofread, others that gave helpful feedback, and many who shared encouraging words related to the impact of this material. There were several who helped with proofreading, including my own mother who spent many hours reading through the original text from 2006 and correcting my many errors (and again with the revision in 2011). As with any written project I am sure our eyes may have still missed typos and errors, but I am grateful for the assistance of several key folks who were willing to correct my many blunders along the way.

I also want to thank my wife who contributed to this material in week seven. She was excited about the opportunity and rose to the challenge several years ago and now is so grateful to know that in this revised and updated version, another audience might benefit from her words of challenge and encouragement. I believe you will enjoy her writing and review of a great work that has benefitted our own marriage. Reflecting back over the past five years affirms once again her commitment to what she wrote.

It is with a great deal of satisfaction that I present this book to you as the culmination of many hours of preparation and contemplation on God's Ten Commandments. I pray you are challenged as I have been to renew your passion for obeying God's Ten Commandments. Enjoy the journey. God bless you for desire to learn more, to love more, and to live more for Christ.

Introduction

You are about to embark on a fascinating journey through the Ten Commandments. It will be fascinating not because of the level of experience with which I have written these daily devotionals, but because I honestly believe that you will gain a new appreciation and life application for each of God's commands. You will be challenged to allow God's Word to guide every aspect of your life; from your daily walk with God to raising your children; from your entertainment choices to your marriage; from your worship of God to your satisfaction in Christ alone. You will discover on your journey that the Ten Commandments are the Measure of God's Love for us demonstrated through principles that seek to radically change our lives.

The Ten Commandments are not difficult to comprehend. In fact, the teachings are rather elementary as something that kids learn in children's Bible classes. The difficulty comes in application. These Ten Commandments from God touch on life's most basic and prevalent issues. For that reason, we would do well to grasp the truths and principles of these commands of God. In fact, I believe grasping these truths will revolutionize your daily walk with the Lord.

I want to thank you in advance for the opportunity to join with you on this journey. I have been challenged and blessed by the time I have spent in God's Word preparing this material, and I pray the same and more will occur in your own life. In closing, I simply ask you to enjoy the parts where I got it right, forgive the parts where I got it wrong, and as you have opportunity, share with me how God has used these Ten Commandments in your life!

A Selection of New Testament References to the Ten Commandments

Commandment No.	New Testament Verse
1st	"You must love the Lord your God with all your heart, all your soul, and all your mind." Matthew 22:37
2nd	"For we walk by faith, not by sight." 2 Cor. 5:7
3rd	"What union can there be between God's temple and idols? For we are the temple of the living God." 2 Cor. 6:16
4th	"On the first day of the week we gathered to observe the Lord's Supper" Acts 20:7
5th	"You children must always obey your parents, for this is what pleases the Lord." Col. 3:20
6th	"You have heard that it was said to those of old, 'You shall not murder, and whoever murders will be in danger of the judgment. But I say to you that whoever is angry with his brother without a cause shall be in danger of the judgment. And whoever says to his brother, 'RacaRaca!' shall be in danger of the council. But whoever says, 'You fool!' shall be in danger of hell fire." Matthew 5:21,22
7th	"You have heard that it was said to those of old, 'You shall not commit adultery. But I say to you that whoever looks at a woman to lust for her has already committed adultery with her in his heart. Matt. 5:27-28
8th	"The commandments against adultery and murder and stealing and coveting - and any other commandment - are all summed up in this one

	commandment; Love your neighbor as yourself." Romans 13:9
9th	"So put away all falsehood and 'tell your neighbor the truth' because we belong to each other.' Eph. 4:25
10th	"I would have never know that coveting is wrong if the law had not said, 'Do not covet.'" Rom. 7:7

(Source: Bill Bright, *Written by the Hand of God*. p. 34)

THE MEASURE OF LOVE

CHAPTER ONE

The Measure of our Devotion

The Measure of our Devotion

Each day will begin with a Daily Scripture Passage. I encourage you to take time to read the daily passage because it will serve as the foundation on which the day's devotional will be built. Following the Daily Scripture Passage will be the Thought to Consider. This will help focus your mind on the teaching of the day and help to set the framework for the day's teaching.

Daily Scripture Passage: Exodus 19:3-6
"Then Moses went up to God, and the LORD called to him from the mountain and said, "This is what you are to say to the house of Jacob and what you are to tell the people of Israel: 'You yourselves have seen what I did to Egypt, and how I carried you on eagles' wings and brought you to myself. Now if you obey me fully and keep my covenant, then out of all nations you will be my treasured possession. Although the whole earth is mine, you will be for me a kingdom of priests and a holy nation.' These are the words you are to speak to the Israelites."

Thought to Consider: Preparing for the Presence of God

As we begin our study of the Ten Commandments I believe it is crucial for us to prepare for the presence of God. That is the focus behind our passage for today - to prepare God's people for an encounter that would from that point forward guide their steps. You may have noticed that this passage appears on the back of the book. It is the foundational principle for how we read God's Ten Commandments. God spoke these initial words recorded in Exodus 19 to give Moses and the people of God the context of what was to come. The commandments that would follow were not harsh rules from a dictator, but the Measure of God's Love and provision for His people.

Growing up I can remember that Sundays were always a rush. The pants that fit a few weeks ago were now an inch shorter and the shirt that matched had apparently "walked off by itself" (as my mother would say). Inevitably, an argument would break out among me and two brothers and Sunday morning was once again hectic. The rush seemed to take on a different face as I got older. No longer did I have trouble finding clothes that fit, it was just that I had a more difficult time crawling out of bed in time to get those clothes on and make it to church. Becoming a teenager somehow included a hibernation instinct that required twelve plus hours of sleep (I'm still trying to shake that teenage sleep instinct many years later). So while the chaos of Sunday mornings changed, I still found myself rushing to church. As I look back on those years of my life I realize that all too often I was coming into God's house frazzled and unprepared for His presence. While I was there physically, little thought and prayer had gone into preparing for His presence. Now I would love to be able to say that today my entrance into God's house is always preceded by a peaceful time of prayer and soul searching, but the challenge of today's devotional is equally applied to my own life as I imagine it is for yours. But beyond Sunday mornings, our challenge for preparing for the presence of God applies to every opportunity we have for an encounter with a holy God.

Preparation was central to God's plan of giving the Ten Commandments.

Preparation was central to God's plan of giving the Ten Commandments. As we come to these opening verses of Exodus 19, it is as if God is saying, "Moses, before you give My people these commands, before anything else, will you please remind them that I bore them on eagles' wings?"

In the face of slavery; in the face of mistreatment, and in the face of great trial, He bore them on eagle's wings. What a wonderful statement to remind the people of His love and relationship to them! It is in the context of Exodus 19:3-6 that we must read the Ten Commandments. These are not harsh, restrictive, and brutal commands from our Heavenly Father. Instead, in the context of Exodus 19, we see these commandments as the extension of His love and provision for His people.

God's Word says that He will bear us up on eagle's wings. That means we will fly higher than we could have ever imagined if we will simply trust in His commands and live according to His provisions. The context of these verses points to one thing - the giving of the Ten Commandments.

As we move through this material together you will have the opportunity to study the Ten Commandments in great detail. I pray that these devotionals will be for *your* benefit. You are certainly welcome to read multiple sections per sitting, but this material was written with the goal of reading just one per day and allowing that material to soak in and challenge you. Will you commit to this time each day in order to grow in your walk with the Lord? I truly believe that as a result of the time in this material, and especially God's

Word, you will begin to understand these commands as the Measure of His Love!

During our study of the Ten Commandments, there will be sections where questions will be available as a follow-up to the material. If you choose to use these questions, they will serve to reinforce the day's material through a time of reflection and application. Enjoy this study as you grow in your walk with Christ.

Take a moment to reflect back on Exodus 19:3-6. How does Exodus 19:3-6 affect your perception of the Ten Commandments?

How could the Ten Commandments allow you to soar higher than ever before?

- In your relationship with God?

- In your relationship with your spouse or parents?

- In your work environment?

- Other:

What trials have you endured over the past year?

How has God carried you through those trials?

How are you trusting God today?

ꕥ

The Measure of our Devotion

Daily Scripture Passage: Matthew 22:37-38
Jesus replied: " 'Love the Lord your God with all your heart and with all your soul and with all your mind. This is the first and greatest commandment."
1 John 5:2-3
"This is how we know that we love the children of God: by loving God and carrying out his commands. This is love for God: to obey his commands. And his commands are not burdensome"

Thought to Consider: Do I love God with all my heart, soul, and mind?

5	3			7				
6			1	9	5			
	9	8					6	
8				6				3
4			8		3			1
7				2				6
	6					2	8	
			4	1	9			5
				8			7	9

Sudoku is one of the many puzzle book choices found in most newsstands today. Though it has been played since about 1990 in some parts of the world, it has enjoyed quite a swell in attention here in America over the past ten years. I must say that my original perception of this game was that it was a pointless, time-wasting game. However, on the many flights of my mission trip to Indonesia during the summer of 2006, I noticed a few individuals sitting around me with Sudoku puzzle books. I did not understand the point of the game and it certainly did not look appealing to me. Besides, anything resembling math did not look like an enticing hobby to me! But that is until my mother explained how it works. In the days that followed my wife and I quickly worked our way through several books. And though we have now moved on to other things, we did discover several years ago that something called Sudoku could be a challenge and a lot of fun too!

Regardless of what you might do for enjoyment, the truth is the same for all of us - we all desire happiness and joy! It is certainly alright to find joy and happiness in this life that God has given us! But ultimately we must find our core happiness and joy in only one way - through obeying and serving God. As a believer in the Lord Jesus Christ I should find joy in serving and being obedient to His will. If that is not the case, then I need to do a heart check. Several years ago, in the church where we were serving, we preceded this study of the Ten Commandments with a study of 1 John. Within that book we see this principle of serving with joy taught again and again. We must find joy in serving!

As we prepare for our study of the Ten Commandments, this truth is critical to understand. The first and greatest commandment is to love God supremely. That is our charge and our challenge as children of God. Everything that we strive to be and to do as believers in the Lord Jesus Christ is summed up in this one passage and can be summarized in that simple way - love God supremely. If I desire to be closer in my walk with Christ, then I have only one obligation - to love Him with my heart, soul, and mind. If my daily struggles are overshadowing my faith, then I must turn to Christ and love him with my heart, soul, and mind. If I allow that alone to be the focus of my relationship with Christ, then I will discover true contentment in Christ alone.

The first and greatest commandment is to love God supremely.

These introductory devotionals have one goal - to help you to continue to prepare your heart for receiving God's Ten Commandments in a completely new way, not as rules and restrictions, but as the Measure of His Love for you. I pray that today as you work through the verses as well as the questions that follow, that you will continue to see God's love shining clearly through the Ten Commandments.

Fact to Consider: "The Ten Commandments, simple and profound as they are, are impossible for any of us to keep. We are imperfect humans who hopelessly fail to live up to God's standards in our own self-effort."
Bill Bright, "Written by the Hand of God."

Has your obedience to God been driven by "self-effort", as Bill Bright says above, or a deep for love for God? How so?

In what areas of your life do you need to demonstrate your love for God? Your heart? Your soul? Your mind?

How would your life be different if you viewed God's commands through the lens of His great love for you?

Do you love the Lord your God with all your heart, soul, and mind? If not, where do you need to grow?

The Measure of our Devotion

Daily Scripture Passage: Exodus 20:2-3
"I am the LORD your God, who brought you out of Egypt, out of the land of slavery. "You shall have no other gods before me."

Thought to Consider: The Priority of God

As we discussed in the previous section, the Measure of our Love for God is determined by our willingness to follow His commands. As we begin today with our study of the first command, allow me to set the stage by sharing the theme for this chapter's material: *The Measure of our Devotion.* As you know, the title of the book is "The Measure of Love". But within each chapter is a subtitle designed to help you to understand how that particular commandment is the Measure of God's Love. Commandment number one is a Measure of our Devotion to God as we are instructed to have "no other gods before Him."

God's word to us in the Ten Commandments begins in Exodus 20:2 where He says, "I am the Lord your God, who brought you out of Egypt, out of the land of slavery." These words speak to priority - the priority of God as *our Lord.* As Ron Mehl shares in his book *The Tender Commandments*, "The greatest challenge I face every day of my life is probably the very one that you face every day...maintaining a close, personal, growing relationship with Jesus Christ. It is keeping him first." Adherence to the Ten Commandments, and any of the other commands of God, hinges on maintaining a close, personal, growing relationship with Christ. Apart from this the commands are burdensome.

Adherence to the Ten Commandments, and any of the other commands of God, all hinge on maintaining a close, personal, growing relationship with Christ.

You may not know that the Ten Commandments are not only found in Exodus 19, but are repeated in their entirety in Deuteronomy 5. Following the Ten Commandments in Deuteronomy, we read in the following chapter a declaration of commitment that has resounded for centuries. Deut. 6:4 says, "Hear, O Israel: The Lord our God, the Lord is one." As we come to the Ten Commandments we are challenged to do a heart check. Is God truly our priority? We learn in Deuteronomy that the Lord our God, the Lord is ONE. There can be no other that holds that position. We must understand that as we

begin to study and attempt to better understand the life application of God's law, that we must first and foremost declare that we love God and know that He is One.

Consider how our love for Him alone affects the remaining commandments. If God is your priority, will you worship idols? Certainly not. If God is your priority, will you misuse his name? Certainly not. If God is your priority, will keeping the Sabbath be difficult? Absolutely not. Throughout the Ten Commandments we learn that this pivotal issue will affect all of the remaining commands. "I am the Lord *your* God."

On my left hand is a wedding ring. This wedding ring does not make me married. Rather, it is the symbol and witness to everyone that I *am* married. In the same way, my love for God's laws does not make me saved or in a relationship with God. That love is the symbol and witness of a relationship that has already begun. For the people of Israel, they needed to be reminded of their relationship with God before they heard any other commands. What God requires is not empty service or sacrifice, but faithful obedience. For the people of Israel, they needed to first and foremost set their focus on God alone. He was the Lord their God.

Today we need that same reminder. Who is our God? If He is the Lord Almighty, then that truth will affect all of the remaining commands. His commands will not seem burdensome. Instead they will be seen as the Measure of His Love! May we be challenged today to demonstrate the measure of our devotion to Him!

If you are married, what are some ways that demonstrate to others your marriage relationship?

In the same manner, what are some ways that your life is demonstrating to others your relationship with God?

"You are the Lord my God." How can your life reflect that as your statement of commitment today?

The Measure of our Devotion

Daily Scripture Passage: Matthew 6:33
"But seek first the kingdom of God and His righteousness, and all these things shall be added to you."

Thought to Consider: Demonstrating Faithfulness Each Day

Through the preparation and study time that originally went into writing these devotionals I discovered some really good resources on the Ten Commandments that still remain on my shelf today. One of those resources is Bill Bright's book, *Written by the Hand of God.* In his book, Bright tells about a group of people in the town of Chaiyaphum, Thailand. In that town, the people worshiped a large rock right in the center of town. Whenever they faced a difficult situation they would actually come to this huge rock for help. At the huge rock they would consult the man who served as the "interpreter" for the rock. This man was completely loyal to his position, never leaving his post as interpreter for the rock. There were Christian missionaries in the area, but none dared share Christ with the man at the rock because of their fear of the man and the townspeople. One day a Campus Crusade for Christ missionary was bold enough to sit down with the man and share the gospel and, to the amazement of everyone, the man accepted Christ. When invited to a follow-up session the man brought his entire family. For the first time in this man's adult life he put Christ first over any rock or idol.

You might say, "How absurd to consider standing by a rock and serving as its interpreter for all those years!" That might be our response, but are our actions any less despicable when we turn to the more polished and refined idols of our day?

In the church where I serve, we adopted an annual theme in 2011 entitled "Filled to Flow: Filled with Christ to flow out with hope for our world." There were two priorities found in that theme. First, we were to commit to putting Christ first. Second, we were to allow that to then lead us outward as we demonstrated our faith in real acts of service. But it is that first aspect that I want us to consider within this context, that of putting God first. That idea is based on Matthew 6:33 which says, "Seek first His kingdom and His righteousness, and all these things will be added unto you." (NKJV) Our focus was first to be on Christ.

The first commandment is about the focus of our worship. It is the "who" of our worship. The test for determining the *who* of your worship is rather simple. Simply ask yourself right now, "What consumes my mind above all else?" Sure the stresses of your job and raising kids (even grown kids) fill your mind, but when you get down to the core of what consumes you, is it a kingdom first mindset?

What I have learned in my walk with the Lord is that this is one of those "day to day" kinds of things. While I may have been faithfully seeking Him yesterday, that does not guarantee or determine how I'm going to seek Him today. Each day I must determine to "seek first His kingdom."

Our task is not to consider what great change we need to make *tomorrow* in order to seek first His kingdom. Instead, consider *this* day what you can do to better demonstrate your complete devotion and allegiance to God alone. Today, say to Him, "There are no other gods before You!"

Our worship may not be focused on a large rock at the center of town, but what has turned our eyes off of the one true God? That will be different for all of us, but the task is the same - worship God alone.

What are some ways that you have demonstrated a "Kingdom First" mindset in your own life?

Matthew 6:33 teaches that if we will seek first the kingdom "all these things will be added unto you." What are some of those "things" that are taking first place in your life rather than seeking Christ?

What action steps do you need to take today in order to live out a "Kingdom First" life?

The Measure of our Devotion

Daily Scripture Passage: Ecclesiastes 12:1
Remember your Creator in the days of your youth, before the days of trouble come and the years approach when you will say, "I find no pleasure in them"

Thought to Consider: Worshiping Before Difficulty Comes

Do you ever have moments of "brilliance"? Do you have those moments when you seem to handle things better than you normally do or respond in a way that even impresses yourself? I think most of us have those moments of brilliance that we wish would appear much more often.
In much the same way, I have those moments of brilliant worship. It is a time of worship that propels me forward in my growth in Christ. I often find that it is these times that I draw on when my worship is not as sweet as before.

Now let's just be honest with each other today and take off the "holy mask". When I come to worship on Sundays there are those times when I feel like I'm singing more to fill the room than to praise my Heavenly Father. Have you been there too? It might be distractions or fatigue or many other things, but for whatever reason I feel as though my worship is not as sweet as it has been before. But praise God there are also those wonderful times when I am truly swept up in the worship experience. I lose myself in the praise of His glory. My troubles, my stress, my weariness, all fade away as I praise His name. O how I long for those times to be more and more frequent!

In today's passage we read of a challenge spoken as words of wisdom for our lives. I believe this passage can speak to our worship. It is a challenge for us to come to our Creator in worship of Him before we grow older and find no joy in our days. But I think we can also see in this passage the correlation to worshiping before trouble comes in our lives. Allow me to explain. There is no doubt that with age comes responsibility and often stress. While most of us would not want to be 15 again, most all of us would love to have the stress load (with the exception of school) of a 15 year old. In that light, we might read this passage like this, "Remember your Creator in the days when life is much easier, before the hard days come and the years approach when you say, 'I find no pleasure in them.'"

The Measure of our Love for Him, according to the book of 1 John, is following His commands. I believe the Measure of our Love for Him is also demonstrated in our worship, that above all else we remember God. We remember Him in the good times. We remember Him in the difficult times. We remember Him, not just as a youth, but as we grow older and our responsibilities and trials grow as well.

The first commandment speaks to our priorities, and I believe we discover our priorities most when we check to see if we remember God only in the good times, or whether we look to Him at *all* times.

If I am going to declare today that He alone is God and that I serve no other, that fact becomes clearest in the face of my own trials and difficulties. As our passage for today challenges us to realize, I *can* find joy in my days of trouble if *He* is my God. I *can* find peace in the midst of turmoil if *He* is my God. That's the kind of faith I desire and the kind of faith that I witnessed in a dear family of our church in the week this devotional was written. This family experienced peace in the midst of great turmoil because He is their God.

If I am going to declare today that He alone is God and that I serve no other, that fact becomes clearest in the face of my own trials and difficulties.

Where are you placing your trust today? Are you remembering Him today before the days of trial come? As you consider that, pray for those within your church family who are in that day of trial, that they would lean on the love of our Heavenly Father, and experience His peace!

The Measure of our Devotion

Daily Scripture Passage: John 6:35
Then Jesus declared, "I am the bread of life. He who comes to me will never go hungry, and he who believes in me will never be thirsty."

Thought to Consider: Finding our satisfaction in Christ alone.

"Obey your thirst". In the mid 1990's, Sprite launched that phrase as their promotional slogan. Are you thirsty? Then obey your thirst by drinking one of our cold Sprites! It seems to have been a rather effective campaign because it is still in use today.

We all have a "thirst" for something. Whether it is a soft drink or a new car, we all have a desire for satisfaction in the things that are all around us. But the challenge for us as believers is to apply God's Word to our lives and as a result find our satisfaction in Him alone.

Satisfaction is defined as "a fulfillment of a need or a want". In our passage for today we discover that if we come to the bread of life we will never hunger, nor will we thirst. Jesus is the end all for our thirst and endless hunger for things that will leave us empty.

Jesus is the end all for our thirst and endless hunger for things that will leave us empty.

We read a similar verse earlier in John 4:14, "but whoever drinks of the water that I shall give him will never thirst. But the water that I shall give him will become in him a fountain of water springing up into everlasting life." In our deepest longings and searching we discover that Christ truly is the fulfillment of every thirst we have. We discover that our satisfaction can be found in Christ alone.

In this chapter, we have been talking about the command for us to have "no other gods before him." As we come to this final day of our devotions in chapter one, I believe we can discover what this command boils down to. If today we determine that we can find satisfaction nowhere else but in Christ, we will keep our eyes focused on Him.

When my satisfaction is in Christ alone, then I trust His commands.

> When my satisfaction is in Christ alone, then I understand that those commands come from my loving heavenly Father.
>
> When my satisfaction is in Him alone, I will determine today that my eyes will remain focused on Him.

Through the busyness and distractions of my day I long to keep Him at the center of everything that I am and find my satisfaction in Him alone. Can you imagine the difference that this would make in your walk with Christ? Think back over your journey of faith. How many headaches could you have avoided if you would have been convinced that your satisfaction would be found only in Christ? If I am convinced of that, then I will invest in my faith daily. I will desire over everything else to know Christ more, to love Him more, and to serve Him more faithfully each and every day. Why? Because I realize that He is the source of my satisfaction. There is no need to invest my focus anywhere else.

The command to have no other gods before Him would become a given. Why would I place anything or anyone before the very ONE that gives me complete satisfaction? How ridiculous to even consider it! I pray that we are *that* convinced of putting nothing or no one before our God. He is worthy to be praised! He is worthy of obedience! He is worthy!

What is the biggest obstacle for you to find your satisfaction in Christ alone?

What are those things for which you thirst that keep you from coming to the true fountain - God?

What step can you take today to demonstrate your complete satisfaction in Christ alone?

What is God teaching you in this passage and this commandment?

*New section added to the revised version of this book.

Connecting with the Commandments
WEEK ONE

Over lunch one day I was listening to a friend share about goals that he had in his work life and how he had been so fortunate to receive the job that he had. Then, in an almost awkward transition he said, "This is totally unrelated to that but I need to ask, 'How can my wife and I come together in our relationship with Christ?'"

Though most would not be as open as my friend was on that day, I believe this is an issue facing many couples and families within our churches. We are grateful for the opportunity to worship together in a great church, but that time of worship often does not translate into an intimate relationship with God that is openly discussed within the marriage relationship. That is the objective of this newly added section to the revised and updated version of "The Measure of Love".

As I anticipated re-releasing this material in a new context, this new component was an aspect that God laid on my heart several months ago. So in the "Connecting with the Commandments" section, you will be invited to enter into a family devotional time. Your family may be you, your spouse, and children. At this point your family may be just you and your spouse. Still, for others of you that now live alone, this will be a time when you may invite family members over to share in this time. As they come for a visit, invite them to share together with you the activities and reflection within the "Connecting with the Commandments" pages.

This time with your family will not come easily. You will have to work to allot time in your weekly schedule to accomplish this time. However, the investment of spending time discussing God's Word and its implications for your life and your family's life will be well worth the commitment of your time.

As I often share with those who will be leading in teaching roles, the material is what you make of it! I encourage Sunday School teachers, small group leaders, and pastors to always make any resource they come across one that reflects their personality. That is the strength of any presentation – that it is yours! So take what I have written, adapt it to your personality or the dynamic of your family, and make this material your very own.

Connecting with the Commandments
WEEK ONE

Setting: Invite your children to join you around the table or in your family room. One suggested setting for this would be around the table just following your evening meal, even if that is taking place in a restaurant. Since there is only one connection time per week, there is flexibility on when you decide to do this time together.

Opening Activity for Families with Older Children:
Invite your kids to share what they believe is the #1 movie of all time. Ask them to share why they think that is the best movie ever. After they share, tell them a movie from when you were young that was the top movie of the time, and explain why you think that movie was so great.

(The material now changes to a conversational tone that can be read directly to your children)
Transition from Opening Activities: In the same way that you say a movie is a #1 movie, what we're going to talk about for the next few minutes is the fact that God calls us to put a rank on Him. And just as you shared with us your #1 movie of all time, what we are going to see in this time is that God calls on us to give Him that spot in our lives – He is to be #1. Nothing should ever compete for His spot as the best or the most important.
So to help us see that today, we're going to look at a few verses that we (your parents) have been studying this week in our reading time.

I'm going to read the verse in an easy-to-understand Bible version.
Exodus 20:2-3 (New International Reader's Version)
2 "I am the Lord your God. I brought you out of Egypt. That is the land where you were slaves. 3 "Do not put any other gods in place of me.
Picking Something Else: Let's imagine for a minute that we have gone out to eat together. The waitress brings your plate of food and on it you see collard greens, rice, okra, and liver. Is there anything on that plate that you would like to trade for something else? How about French fries? Would you like to trade the liver or collard greens for French fries? What about chicken tenders rather than that liver? You might like one or two of those items on the plate, but if you were given the option, you would probably want to put something else in the place of several of those items!

But as we think about how that relates to our verse today, what we discover from the Bible is that nothing can take the place of God! We can't trade Him for something else.

The Bible says that that we are to put no other gods before him.

What does it mean "to put no other gods before him."
Actually what this is saying is that we should not allow anything to take our focus off of loving God. We may never think of following another god, but we often put other things before God by the way we live. And what the Bible teaches us is that nothing should take that top spot from God!

What are some things that you think will take our focus off of God?

___ Anger towards someone. ___ Being selfish.
___ Not listening in church. ___ Our belongings.

There are lots of things that can take our focus off of God. But our passage today says that we need to make sure that He is always #1 in our lives.

Setting the Record
The MINI Cooper is a car designed for 4 people. It is so small that some even say that it's hard to fit 4 adults in it. It has a backseat that is almost too small for 2 adults. So it is a small car.

How many adults do you think could cram into that car to set a record? 10? 12?
Well, believe it or not, in December 2010, the Guinness World Record was set with 26 adults, in a 2 door Mini Cooper! Now that's quite a record!

Just as it took a lot of work to achieve that No. 1 spot in the Mini Cooper challenge, so we will have to work to make sure we keep God in that No. 1 spot in our lives and in our family!

Commitment and Prayer: So to help us keep God in that No. 1 spot in our family, let's start out by praying together and thanking God for loving us!

THE MEASURE OF LOVE

CHAPTER TWO

The Measure of our Worship

Welcome to chapter two of our study of the Ten Commandments. I want to thank you for allowing me the opportunity to join together with you on this journey through the Commandments. For those of you with children still at home, I hope that you were able to pause at the conclusion of the previous week to spend time together connecting with the Commandment. This new section was added for the purpose of gathering families together around God's Word, and since this devotional book is geared primarily towards an older audience, I hope this new section with kids in mind will allow this to be an opportunity for all of the family to be challenged by God's Word. I look forward to hearing your stories about how this new section became a meaningful time for you and your family.

It is my prayer that these devotionals will be a time that you will look forward to each day as we study together. As you know, we will study one commandment per chapter, with the exception of commandments eight and nine which will be studied in one chapter. As with any in-depth study, the temptation will be prevalent to lose steam as we move through these nine chapters. My own book reading often resembles my desire to exercise. I begin strong and fade over the coming days. I want to challenge you to make a commitment to persevere through this wonderful study. I have a deeper respect for the application of the Ten Commandments as a result of the time I have invested in studying each one. I believe the same can be true for you if you will commit to this time through reading each day's devotional.

The Measure of our Worship

Daily Scripture Passage: Exodus 20:4
"You shall not make for yourself a carved image—any likeness of anything that is in heaven above, or that is in the earth beneath, or that is in the water under the earth"

Thought to Consider: Drawing our Eyes off the Real Thing

As we begin the second commandment, we quickly discover that the first and second commands are very closely related. At first glance, these two commands almost seem repetitive. But the line that I have discovered that distinguishes these two commands is that the first command speaks to the "who" of our worship and the second command speaks to the "how" of worship.

Those at the bottom of Mount Sinai erected a statue and began worshiping a "thing" rather than God. The "how" of their worship (focusing on man-made idols) was completely wrong, and it therefore affected the "who" of their worship. God's desire is that our focus be solely on Him because He is a jealous God. To focus our attention on any "thing" breaks the second commandment and, in turn, breaks the first.

I believe a step in understanding the application of this commandment in our lives is defining worship. I have seen it defined by dividing it in this way: "worth-ship". We are determining what is *worthy* of our devotion, and one of the best ways to measure our devotion is how we use our time. That will show us more than anything else the measure of our love for God, or the measure of our idolatry. In the context of the second command, their idolatry was an image or statue.

Our lives are inundated with images. An image is often used as a reflection of the real thing. In relation to the second command, that image draws our eyes away from the real thing. Anything that attempts to draw our eyes away from the real thing fits the category of idolatry. Considering it in that way helps us to understand how our entertainment, leisure time, wealth (or lack of wealth), can all fill the role of idolatry. Idols in biblical times always drew the eyes of the worshippers off of the real thing. While we may not construct a stone or golden idol, our eyes are drawn away even more so than those at the base of Mount Sinai.

God knows that our hearts are inclined to worship the things around us just as those at the bottom of the mountain were worshiping an idol even as the command was delivered. Because of this, He gives us this command for *our* good so that we might keep our eyes on the real thing.

Do you know that even our worship can draw our eyes off of the real thing? The Pharisees were certainly guilty of this in New Testament times. Their strict rules and regulations may have started because of their love for God, but that is far from the relationship that we see during Jesus' ministry. Rather than focusing their eyes on the *subject* of their rules, they became fascinated with the creation of and adherence to more and more rules. Our worship cannot be limited to a particular style of worship, whether in a hymn or praise chorus. To do so would mirror the actions of the Pharisees, fascinated with the created rather than the Creator. To declare that I cannot worship through hymns or that I cannot worship through choruses of praise demonstrates that my eyes have truly been taken away from the real thing.

Our calling is to worship in "spirit and in truth" (Jn 4:24). May the methods and traditions of our worship (the "how" of our worship) not distract us from the most important - the "who" of our worship.

What has traditionally drawn your eyes "off of the real thing" throughout your journey of faith?

We touched on a sensitive issue today - methods of worship. Why does one worship style help you to worship more than another?

Do you think that this preference has determined what worship is for you?

How might this preference become an idol?

What is God teaching you today?

The Measure of our Worship

Daily Scripture Passage: Habakkuk 2:20
"But the LORD is in His holy temple. Let all the earth keep silence before Him."

Thought to Consider: Enjoying the Splendor of God

There are certain writers that seem to have a way of teaching that communicates the message so clearly and in a way that you may have never considered it before. Those tend to become your favorite authors. For me, John Piper has been one of those authors that I have respected for many years. While I do not hold all of the convictions held within his books, his way of teaching captivates me. He is a wonderful writer. When I considered the theme of worship, I knew John Piper would be a worthy source. Much of today's material is based on one of his sermon's posted on his website (noted at the end of today's devotional).

To be holy means to be separate. Throughout Scripture we see this principle applied to holy ground (Ex. 19:6), holy assemblies (Ex. 12:16), holy garments (Ex. 28:2), holy promises (Ps. 105:42), holy scriptures (2 Tim. 3:15), holy hands (1 Tim. 2:8), holy faith (Jude 20), and many other examples. As John Piper says, "Almost anything can become holy if it is separated from the common and devoted to God." But when we speak of the holiness of God, the idea is totally different. By just the mention of the name God we understand that His nature is separate from all. He is holy.

In our desire to express the splendor of God we soon realize that our language falls short of reaching His magnificence. In the end, it causes us to reflect on the words of Habakkuk 2:20, "But the Lord is in his holy temple; let all the earth be silent before him." As I contemplate God's holiness, I find myself drawn more to silence because I realize my unworthiness to even speak His name in a way that adequately describes Him. And yet God calls us to come into His presence, praising Him in all of His splendor and to desire to know of His holiness. While my natural inclination might be to simply stand in silence, God desires our praise. What an incredible thought! My worship, as limited and imperfect as it is, is what God desires.

So how does that affect our walk and how does it relate to the second commandment?

1. It changes how we worship and relate to Him.
With a reverence for God's holiness we would never knowingly substitute anything that would take away from our worship of a holy God. So as we come into a place of worship we realize the great importance of preparing our hearts for His presence, removing anything that might distract us from worshiping Him in all of His holiness. As we discussed in the previous devotional, an idol is anything that draws our eyes off of the real thing. In response, we determine to enjoy the splendor of God and allow nothing to draw our eyes off of Him!

2. It reminds us of the foolishness of worshiping anything other than a holy God.
This relates to the second command because it emphasizes the preposterous resolution to worship anything other than an infinitely holy God. If I can truly begin to understand the splendor of Almighty God, it should compel me to worship Him in spirit and in truth - determined to never replace my worship for Him with a focus on any thing or person.

Being captivated by the splendor of God ought to affect our worship. I pray that as we reflect on the second commandment in this chapter, that your worship on Sunday will be intently focused on Him alone, without a concern for the benefit it may bring to you. Just enjoy the splendor of God!

(Resource for today's devotional: John Piper's Sermon *Holy, Holy, Holy is the Lord of Hosts* found at http://www.desiringgod.org)

ॐ

The Measure of our Worship

Daily Scripture Passage: John 21:11-14
[11] Simon Peter went up and dragged the net to land, full of large fish, one hundred and fifty-three; and although there were so many, the net was not broken. [12] Jesus said to them, "Come and eat breakfast." Yet none of the disciples dared ask Him, "Who are You?"—knowing that it was the Lord. [13] Jesus then came and took the bread and gave it to them, and likewise the fish. [14] This is now the third time Jesus showed Himself to His disciples after He was raised from the dead.

Revelation 3:20
"Behold, I stand at the door and knock. If anyone hears My voice and opens the door, I will come in to him and dine with him, and he with Me."

Thought to Consider: Reservations to Dine

Fine woodworking and elegant iron work, pristine lighting and floral arrangements, plush seating and polished tables - these all describe the restaurant to which you are invited tonight. On the menu will be a freshly prepared, exquisitely planned meal that will feed your eyes as much as your stomach. It is the restaurant that all of the papers are talking about. The meals are unlike anything else in town, and you have been invited to come and dine. How incredible is this opportunity! Most would be willing to wait for weeks just to have the opportunity and you have been personally invited by the restaurant owner.

In anticipation of this big night you eat very little for lunch. Besides, you want to be ready to truly enjoy this meal tonight. But on your way to the restaurant you cannot deny your hunger. Maybe the light lunch wasn't such a good idea after all. As you walk down the street towards the restaurant you spot a hot dog cart on the street corner - the kind you see in big cities. There the elderly man is selling hot dogs that have rolled and heated most of the day. Incredibly, the temptation is strong as you smell the onions and chili. What would normally not captivate your nose suddenly draws you in. You stop, purchase a hot dog, and enjoy your evening meal right there by the smell of traffic and trash.

What do you do now? You certainly cannot go into the restaurant now, having filled yourself up on a street corner hot dog. What were you thinking?

You realize that the chance of offending the cook and restaurant owner with your lack of appetite is just too great. You turn and walk back towards your car, full but hardly satisfied.

This may sound like a ridiculous story. Who would stop by a hot dog cart when they know they are about to eat in the finest of restaurants? Maybe you are cluing in on my analogy here. You see, this is exactly what we all do when we substitute anything for the worship of God. Anything other than God Himself is nothing but a cheap, unsatisfying fill that robs you of the opportunity to dine with the Father Himself.

In our verse for today we read an interesting passage where the disciples were invited to have breakfast with Jesus. Can you imagine receiving that invitation? Can you then imagine saying to Jesus, "No...we've already eaten. We chewed on a granola bar while we were out in the boat." That day they did not choose a cheap substitute, but had the opportunity to dine with God Himself.

Elsewhere in Scripture we see this invitation to dine with God. In Revelation 3:20 we read that if we open the door to Him, He will come in and eat with us - an image of intimate fellowship.

As we continue our study of the Ten Commandments, consider today how you are accepting a cheap substitute for an opportunity to dine with the Father. How has the imagery of today's story played out in your daily life? Accept the invitation to dine with him!

Using the story from today's devotional, how can you apply that to a time in your life?

Take a moment to consider a cheap substitute that you have accepted at some time in your life.

If you were invited to that breakfast with Jesus, what would you talk about?

How do you think God feels when we reject his invitation to come and dine with Him?

What is God teaching you today?

ꕥ

The Measure of our Worship

Daily Scripture Passage: John 4:4-15
4 *But He needed to go through Samaria.*
5 *So He came to a city of Samaria which is called Sychar, near the plot of*
ground that Jacob gave to his son Joseph. 6 *Now Jacob's well was there.*
Jesus therefore, being wearied from His journey, sat thus by the well. It
was about the sixth hour. 7 *A woman of Samaria came to draw water. Jesus*
said to her, "Give Me a drink." 8 *For His disciples had gone away into the*
city to buy food. 9 *Then the woman of Samaria said to Him, "How is it that*
You, being a Jew, ask a drink from me, a Samaritan woman?" For Jews
have no dealings with Samaritans.
10 *Jesus answered and said to her, "If you knew the gift of God, and who it*
is who says to you, 'Give Me a drink,' you would have asked Him, and He
would have given you living water."
11 *The woman said to Him, "Sir, You have nothing to draw with, and the*
well is deep. Where then do You get that living water? 12 *Are You greater*
than our father Jacob, who gave us the well, and drank from it himself, as
well as his sons and his livestock?"
13 *Jesus answered and said to her, "Whoever drinks of this water will thirst*
again, 14 *but whoever drinks of the water that I shall give him will never*
thirst. But the water that I shall give him will become in him a fountain of
water springing up into everlasting life."
15 *The woman said to Him, "Sir, give me this water, that I may not thirst,*
nor come here to draw."

Thought to Consider: The Water that Satisfies

In March of 2006 I had the opportunity to travel to Bunda, Tanzania on a mission trip. In our preparation for the trip, the missions team was told that we would carry two liter-size bottles of water for each day and that we would likely drink both bottles before the day ended. For some of you that might not seem like a big task, but not being one that drinks a lot of *anything* during the day I wondered how I was going to hold that much water. Walking in the heat of the Tanzanian villages I soon learned that consuming that much water was no big task at all. That water truly satisfied! I did not want a soft drink. I did not want lemonade. It was water that I wanted because I knew that it was the only thing that would satisfy.

In our passage for today we read about the woman at the well. The promise to her that day was that Jesus could give water that would satisfy - water that would not involve returning to this well to retrieve it. This was certainly puzzling to the woman because as far as she knew there was no such water. Water did not magically appear out of the faucet in her home. If you wanted water, you had to go and retrieve it. But the water that Jesus spoke of that day would quench a deeper thirst. As the story continues we learn that her life was a complete mess, having experienced five divorces and now living with someone that was not her husband. She was trying desperately to fill a void that only could be quenched through the Living Water of Jesus Christ.

In this chapter, we have been challenged by the second commandment - you shall not make for yourself an idol. We have been challenged to not allow anything to take the place of worshiping God alone. But the motivation for this must be deeply rooted in who we are. We must be convinced like the woman at the well was convinced of this living water. We must be convinced like I was convinced while walking the dirt streets of Tanzania that I needed water. Nothing else could satisfy. We must be convinced that there is only One who will satisfy our deepest longings and thirst - the Living Water that comes through Jesus Christ.

The measure of our worship is not solely determined by the songs that we sing on a Sunday morning. Rather, the measure of our worship is also determined by the focus of our attention in all of the days and hours between those Sunday morning or evening services. Do we allow the water that the world offers through entertainment, fast-paced careers, or a multitude of other things satisfy us? Or do we look to Him alone each and every day?

Today I need to look into my heart and ask, "Are you letting something or someone attempt to fill the satisfaction that is only intended to be filled by God? Are you attempting to replace the satisfaction that can only come from Him by some other means?" If I do not come before Him each and every day giving Him the joys and struggles of my day, then the temptation to turn to a multitude of other things only grows.

How is your worship? Isn't He "worthy" of all that you are? Believe and trust today that your satisfaction can *only* come through Him!

ණ

The Measure of our Worship

Daily Scripture Passage: 2 Corinthians 10:5
"Casting down arguments and every high thing that exalts itself against the knowledge of God, bringing every thought into captivity to the obedience of Christ"

Thought to Consider: Take Captive Every Thought

Do we face the same demise and destruction of more lives, or do we do something about it? That was the decision facing Leroy Homer, CeeCee Lyles, Sandra Bradshaw, Todd Beamer, Mark Bingham, Tom Burnett, Andrew Garcia, Jeremy Glick, and Richard Guadango as they fought back against the hijackers of United Flight 93 on September 11, 2001. The 9/11 Commission Report cites that these individuals played a key role in the plane not reaching its intended target. Instead, the plane crashed in Shanksville, Pennsylvania. As the story has been reported, the captive passengers decided to turn the tables on the hijackers and reclaim the plane.

Most every attempt to substitute a *thing* for God originates as a struggle in our thought life. Thoughts like these creep into our minds:
- Can we really be satisfied in Christ alone (the focus of our devotionals on days 2 & 4)?
- Can the water really keep me from thirsting anymore (because I really feel like I am kind of thirsty right now)?
And in a matter of time we have justified our steps and we are led away from the true source of our satisfaction, replacing it with the created rather than the Creator. It all begins in our thought life.

That is what our passage is speaking to today. In the same way that the passengers of Flight 93 made a daring decision to take captive the hijackers, so we need to do each and every day when we realize that a thought that does not glorify God is attempting to gain an audience in our minds. As soon as we realize that our mind is drawing us toward anger, bitterness, lying, lust, coveting, we must determine to take captive that thought. When we understand that our thought life cannot control who we are, that we have the capacity to take captive that thought life, I believe we can live in freedom.

We will not turn the focus of our worship on any counterfeit thing that presents itself as our "god."

Before entertainment becomes the focus of my worship, that thought must begin in my mind where I seek to justify its truth. Consider also worship attendance. I must justify that missing a worship service this one time is perfectly fine. Soon I begin justifying another missed opportunity for worship and on and on the cycle continues.

At the root of each and every illustration that I could give lies the idol that drives them all - the idol of ME. When we begin to move the idol of ME to the throne, anything can fit the agenda of the kingdom, as long as it serves Me. I believe that is why we learn in Scripture that "pride comes before destruction". Pride is defined as "inordinate self-esteem". That means self-esteem that has gone beyond any reasonable limit. When the idol of ME is on the throne, the decisions that I make go beyond any reasonable limit, and the kingdom is going to fall. As strange as this may sound, we were never designed to rule our own lives. That thought may fly in the face of secular media, but it won't disagree with biblical truth. To live is Christ!

When we begin to move the idol of ME to the throne, anything can fit the agenda of the kingdom, as long as it serves Me.

Taking captive every thought means that I have to realize when a sinful thought or action is coming to mind and stop it at that point. Taking captive every thought means that I have to realize when I am slowly placing the idol of ME on the throne and instead submit to Christ's leadership and allowing Him to lead.

If we truly begin to take captive every thought, I believe we will realize the ignorance of our idolatry. We will begin to understand the awesome God that we serve and allow nothing or no one to take His place.

What is one area of your life that you struggle to "take captive" on a regular basis?

What steps can you take today to "take captive" that thought life so that you can experience victory?

Looking back over your walk with Christ, where have you experienced victory over your thought life so that God was glorified?

Write a prayer relating to today's devotional as a commitment to take captive every thought.

Connecting with the Commandments
WEEK TWO

Opening Activity: "A Story Filled with Distractions"
(Read this story as you begin today and then follow up with questions. Try to read right on through the distractions inserted without stopping to acknowledge them as you read.)
Once upon a time, there was a little girl Honda named Katy. Katy loved taking long walks through Chrysler the woods as she looked at all of the beautiful flowers Ford and listen to Toyota all of the sounds she would hear. But her favorite part Corvette of her walks was when she would arrive at Mustang the little waterfall. There she Dodge would take off her shoes, walk down Mazda into the water and just feel the cold water between Lexus her toes. She always loved those walks in the woods and looks forward to returning very soon!
Questions to follow up on the story filled with distractions...
So what did you think about the story?

What did you quickly notice as I was reading that story?

You probably noticed rather quickly that this was a story filled with all kinds of distractions (things not related to the story). As I was reading, you kept hearing names of cars placed in the story for no good reason. It made it hard to pay attention to the story.
The reason we that we read that story to start out today was to prepare us for our Bible verse which will challenge us to not let anything distract us from God. Just as those car names distracted us from the story we read, so we can let a lot of different things distract us from God.

Note to Parents: Before you read the passage for this week, take a moment to explain that our passage for this week is about who we worship, but it is also about how we worship. God has actually told us things that we are *expected* to do and other things that we are commanded *not* to do.

Scripture Passage: Exodus 20:4
"You shall not make for yourself a carved image—any likeness of anything that is in heaven above, or that is in the earth beneath, or that is in the water under the earth"

Share this story as you explain the passage for today…

A Cheap Substitute: While Michael's family was in Costa Rica in their training to be missionaries they had to learn what it was like to live in another culture. Cars were different, food was different, and even shopping was different. One of the things that they discovered was that a lot of the toys that are so popular here are found in other places as cheap versions of those toys. So instead of really nice toys, a lot of the toys there are cheap versions that just don't last as long as the real thing.

Applying the Story: Just as the Hodge family learned that there were things that you can buy that are not as good as the original, in the same way there are things that can distract us from God that are definitely not as good as the original. Sometimes, instead of loving God we can love things. Sometimes, instead of loving opportunities to be in church we love sports or other entertainment. But nothing should be more important to us than God. Sure we can enjoy sports and things that we love doing. God wants us to love life and being with our friends and family. But those things should never keep us from loving God first.

This week has been about having no idols. When God originally challenged the people to not have idols, He wanted them not to make a little statue that would represent their god. It was something that was really common in that time but God said it was wrong because nothing should be a cheap substitute for God Himself.

God wants us to know HIM and not let anything distract us from Him.

Applying this Commandment to our lives Today

There are not many people today who consider making an idol (a statue to represent God). But lots of times we make things that take the place of God in our lives. If anything is more important to us than God, that has become an idol in our life. So this week, let's think of things that we might be considering more important than God and let's commit to putting those things in their right place – as things we love, but never more than our love for God.

THE MEASURE OF LOVE

CHAPTER THREE

The Measure of our Reverence

The Measure of our Reverence

Daily Scripture Passages:
Exodus 20:7
"You shall not take the name of the LORD your God in vain, for the LORD will not hold him guiltless who takes His name in vain."
John 8:54-59
Jesus answered, "If I honor Myself, My honor is nothing. It is My Father who honors Me, of whom you say that He is your God. Yet you have not known Him, but I know Him. And if I say, 'I do not know Him,' I shall be a liar like you; but I do know Him and keep His word. Your father Abraham rejoiced to see My day, and he saw it and was glad."
Then the Jews said to Him, "You are not yet fifty years old, and have You seen Abraham?"
Jesus said to them, "Most assuredly, I say to you, before Abraham was, I AM."
Then they took up stones to throw at Him; but Jesus hid Himself and went out of the temple, going through the midst of them, and so passed by."

Thought to Consider: Recognizing the Greatness of His Name

Among the gospels, John's gospel has been my favorite for many years. Recently, as I was reading through a portion of the Gospel of John, I noticed that over and over Jesus encountering the religious leaders of the day, many of whom were very disturbed at his teaching and particularly His following. At one point in chapter 8, the Jewish leaders pressed Jesus to reveal His identity. As He often did, He used this as an opportunity to teach them, including teaching them about Abraham rejoicing at the thought of seeing Jesus' day. The religious leaders scoffed at such an idea and said, "You are not yet fifty years old and you have seen Abraham!" To this Jesus replied, "before Abraham was born, I am!" This may seem like a simple statement apart from the context of his quote. But to the religious leaders, this was none other than blasphemy. It was a quote of Exodus 3:14 where God said to Moses, "I AM WHO I AM. This is what you are to say to them". The response to His quote of God's words to Moses was indignation because of the perceived blasphemy. How could this man of Nazareth make such a statement? At His statement they did not form a committee. No, that day they formed a mob, intent on killing this heretic from Nazareth.

We learn a couple of things from the events of that day. First of all, we learn that Jesus truly is equal with God. If He is not equal with God then He is a lunatic for making such a statement, but the evidence of Scripture and history affirms his statement. He truly is God. His statement that day was no great leap of confidence and arrogance. It was simply truth, regardless of how it was received that day.

Secondly, we learn of the great importance the religious elite of the day placed on the name of God. To simply quote a name of God and attach that to oneself was worthy of death. That is in stark contrast to movies like *The DaVinci Code* from several years ago which assigned all types of blasphemous teachings on the name of Jesus and was applauded by secular media for their effort. Oh, that we would again have a great reverence for the name of God; that we would always seek to carry that name in a worthy manner before a lost and dying world. To the religious leaders of Jesus' day, they held a high regard for the name of God. That was demonstrated by the deep felt emotion shown as a reaction to Jesus' remarks.

I must confess that as I read this passage I long for that kind of response when I hear the name of my Lord taken in vain. I long to not treat this as commonplace in our society and to experience just a taste of the deep felt emotion of the religious leaders of that day. I long for a love so deep for my God that the sound of His name being profaned hurts my heart. In this chapter, as we consider the third commandment, I pray that we are challenged to recognize again the greatness of his name, the "name above all names".

Can you think of a television show or movie that you recently watched that profaned God's name?

If you were to catalog the irreverent references to God's name within the programs or movies that you watch, would this be a long list of occurrences? Maybe bringing this to mind will allow us to see the great impact this could have on our sensitivity to the name of God.

How can you honor the name of God this week?

How might you not honor God's name this week?

Your prayer for this week...

The Measure of our Reverence

Daily Scripture Passage: Ephesians 5:15-17
"Be very careful, then, how you live—not as unwise but as wise, making the most of every opportunity, because the days are evil. Therefore do not be foolish, but understand what the Lord's will is."

Thought to Consider: Carrying the Name of Jesus

"The third commandment has far more to do with our walk than our talk." That is what Bill Bright learned while in seminary as his professor opened up the great meaning in this commandment. What he discovered is that the key to this commandment lies in the word "take". As it is used here in this passage, it literally means "to carry or bear". The context of that word would typically be the idea of carrying a load. But when it is applied to this setting, it implies the idea of carrying the name of the Lord wherever we go. What a powerful thought, to think that we carry the name of the Lord wherever we go. As we work, we carry the name of the Lord. As we spend time with our families, we carry the name of the Lord. As we play and enjoy fun times, we carry the name of the Lord. Everywhere, and at all times, we are carrying the name of the Lord.

As we continue reading this commandment we see that we are not to carry the name of the Lord "in vain". To do so means that we remove any value from the name. In other words, we assume the role of carrying an "empty name". Carrying his name is a wonderful gift of the grace of God, but if our lives are not a reflection of the name that we carry, then we are carrying it in vain. We have removed the significance of the name which we carry. Allow me to illustrate it this way. As a young person, as you went out of your home and spent time with your friends you were carrying the family name with you. Your mom or dad might have even said something like, "Remember who you are". As you went out and enjoyed your time with friends, you were representing your family – for good or for bad.

Do you realize that as children of God we have the incredible privilege of carrying the name of the Lord in the same way that we carry the name of another in our last name? We are called Christians - which bears the name of Christ. In the same way that someone would look at me and learn how a Hodge should act, so those around us can look at us and determine how a Christian should act. It is a sobering realization.

In our passage for today we are challenged to, first of all, “be careful how you live - not as unwise but as wise.” The Bible is filled with instructions concerning wise and unwise living (i.e. Prov. 4:10-14, ch.9, 10:8, 14). But the reference of this passage is not just in regards to general behavior, but consistent with Paul’s instructions in Colossians 4:5, that we be wise in our actions towards outsiders. As one author, Andrew Lincoln, states, “To live as a wise person is not just to have knowledge but to have skill in living, to have the sort of perception that authenticates itself in practice.” (There is no doubt that a statement like that is from a Bible professor because the rest of us have to spend a few minutes unpacking exactly what it said.) Lincoln is saying that living wise is not just about a lot of life facts or even Bible facts, it is all about how that knowledge plays itself out in your real world. Do you take what you know and allow it to affect the way that you carry the name?

When I studied our passage in Ephesians for today and understood how the commandment applies in this way, I had to ask myself, “How am I carrying the name? Am I carrying the name in a worthy manner?” Today’s devotional is a challenge to me to make the most of every opportunity. As Paul says in our passage today, we need to look for opportunities to carry the name in a way that would glorify Him.

How could you carry the name in a way that would glorify God in your everyday life?

Would others around you say that you are carrying the name well? If not, how can you help change that perception?

The Measure of our Reverence

Daily Scripture Passage: Luke 6:43-45
"No good tree bears bad fruit, nor does a bad tree bear good fruit. Each tree is recognized by its own fruit. People do not pick figs from thornbushes, or grapes from briers. The good man brings good things out of the good stored up in his heart, and the evil man brings evil things out of the evil stored up in his heart. For out of the overflow of his heart his mouth speaks.

Thought to Consider: Bringing Down the Name

Another marriage down the drain; another child is on the way; so and so was spotted with this person. You have probably read headlines much like these as you wait to check out at the grocery or discount store. Apparently to be popular means to be followed. Countless writers and photographers are out to break the story on the hottest new actor or actress. But do you realize that the one story that magazine writers long for more than any other is the one that will destroy the name of this new actor or actress? They know that it is *that* story that will gain the most attention and circulation. Their goal is to bring down the name of this individual.

Today we are talking about the topic "Bringing Down the Name". I came across this idea in Ron Mehl's book "The Tender Commandments". There Mehl says concerning profaning God's name, "It is nothing less than a denial of His holiness and majesty and power. It is an attempt to somehow pull God down to a common level and make Him equal with me." What Mehl is trying to help us understand in his chapter is that we all understand that God is high and lifted up. He is above all else and is worthy of our praise. Our choruses of praise teach us that God is holy. Therefore, my desire as a child of God ought to be to worship Him and to allow my life to be a testimony of that worship. So as we come to the third of the Ten Commandments, we find a measuring rod for our reverence for God. The question before us is this: Are we bringing down the name?

Let me set the framework for what we are talking about today. When we carelessly use the name of the Lord we are actually bringing down His name. The Bible teaches us that His is the name above all names and that at the name of Jesus every knee will bow. By carelessly using the name of God we

are denying the holiness due His name by associating the Name with the profane. We are disagreeing with the fact that He is holy and altogether separate from anything unholy. This is not a language issue. This is not a vocabulary or environment issue. This is a heart issue. To help us to understand that, I chose Luke 6:42-45 as our passage for today.

In our passage for today, we read about the good and bad tree. One brings forth good fruit and the other results in bad fruit. But the key verse for us today is in vs. 45 where we learn that the overflow of the heart determines what comes out of the mouth. Bringing down the name of the Lord is not a simple mistake or bad habit. According to Scripture, it reveals a greater problem. It is the measure of our love for Him expressed in our words.

As you read today's devotional you may be thinking, "Cursing and using God's name in vain is not a problem for me." If that is the case, then I want to rejoice with you that this is not a struggle in your walk with the Lord. But what we are talking about is not an issue of words as much as it is an issue of the heart. Cursing may not be a struggle in your walk with the Lord, but have you considered the common practice of using substitute words for the name of God like "gosh," "jeez," and so forth. I want to challenge you to see that simply substituting words for the name of God with common slang words does not keep us outside of the parameters of the command. This command is a measure of our reverence for God. To stand as close to the line as possible certainly does not confirm our love for Him.

What is the overflow of your heart? Is it love for Him?

Do you long, more than anything else, to lift up His name? If that is your desire today, then God will be pleased and glorified in your life!

Have you noticed yourself using the name of the Lord in your everyday language in a way that does not honor Him?

The Measure of our Reverence

Daily Scripture Passage: Leviticus 22:32-33
"Do not bring shame on my holy name, for I will display my holiness among the people of Israel. I am the LORD who makes you holy. It was I who rescued you from the land of Egypt, that I might be your God. I am the LORD." NLT

Thought to Consider: Just Another Word, Right?

In his book "Engraved on Your Heart: Living the Ten Commandments Day by Day," Bill Hybels tells the story of when he was just a little boy and on the job with his dad. There he was able to mingle with the grown-ups - the "real" men as he called them. In the midst of working among those men he learned a great deal. Some of what he learned was good, but much of it was not so good. Bill's dad was a dockworker and the language of those down at the dock was as colored as the sunrise. One of those days while he was down at the dock he heard a few four letter words that he thought were interesting, a sort of new vocabulary that he had not heard before. It was just as common to the men as the words in young Bill's vocabulary. Bill was impressed with this new language, and thought it would be a good idea to see if it would work for him.

Bill had an older brother - one of those older brothers that could not be impressed. So attempting to impress his big brother was a daily goal of young Bill. On this night he decided that his new vocabulary would impress big brother, so he let a word fly. Eyes as big as saucers, his brother glared at him in amazement, not saying a word to his younger brother. Bill thought for sure that he had just impressed his brother a great deal. Maybe this new language works.

That night the entire family sat around the table for supper. Bill described it as a Norman Rockwell kind of setting with everyone in their place. Following the meal dad asked what the kids were planning on doing that night. Bill rocked back in his chair and let another one of those words fly to convey the idea of an "I don't care" attitude. Suddenly, his brother did not look as impressed. His sister was staring at him with her mouth wide open. Mom was crying. Dad was on his way towards Bill with a look of anger and wrath. Bill realized his new vocabulary wasn't so good after all.

If you have kids, or can remember being one, there might have been a time when you or your kids explored the limits and may have discovered like Bill Hybels did, that this new language did not belong in your home. You were naïve and curious at the same time. But to take the name of the Lord in vain is a serious sin - one on which the promise of judgment has been attached. If you have committed this sin in ignorance or are becoming too comfortable with a bad vocabulary, confess that sin today and commit to no longer profaning the name of God. Commit to carrying His name in honor. We cannot commit this sin in ignorance any longer.

In our verse for today we are challenged to no longer treat God's name as common and ordinary. Profaning the name of the Lord might not be a great issue for you in your life, but as we consider Leviticus 22:32, I believe we can all stand to do a heart check on how we treat the name. As we prepare for worship each Sunday, have we spent the time preparing our hearts to come before Him? As we come before Him in prayer, are we approaching the throne with submissive hearts and servant attitudes? Or are we more interested in what God is going to do for us? Are we more interested in what is in it for us than what we can offer God in worship and service? I only ask those questions today because I realize as I study this commandment that all too often I approach the Name as all too common and ordinary - two words that should never describe my God.

May we not be ignorant today, like the young Bill Hybels, of the glory of God's name and the great sin of misusing that name. May we treat the Name with great honor and *extra*ordinary respect.

Was there a time in your life when you realized that some words did not belong in your home or in your class? Write about that here...

Has this week's devotionals helped you to see an area in your life where you need to make a change? Maybe you've been like Bill Hybels, using language that you should not.

How can you revere the name of God in your everyday life?

Your prayer for today…

The Measure of our Reverence

Daily Scripture Passage: Philippians 2:5-11
"Let this mind be in you which was also in Christ Jesus, who, being in the form of God, did not consider it robbery to be equal with God, but made Himself of no reputation, taking the form of a bondservant, and coming in the likeness of men. And being found in appearance as a man, He humbled Himself and became obedient to the point of death, even the death of the cross. Therefore God also has highly exalted Him and given Him the name which is above every name, that at the name of Jesus every knee should bow, of those in heaven, and of those on earth, and of those under the earth, and that every tongue should confess that Jesus Christ is Lord, to the glory of God the Father." NKJV

Thought to Consider: A God-Centered Theology

In our home there are two degrees from Anderson College (which is now Anderson University), one that is my degree and the other is my wife's degree. Also at home I have a degree from Southeastern Baptist Theological Seminary. All of these degrees are from accredited schools. That means that an outside agency has affirmed their right to be a university or seminary and to award degrees based on a student's work. Without that accreditation agency's stamp of approval, those degrees would mean very little. They would simply be finely printed paper records of class attendance. But businesses and churches take those degrees seriously because of the integrity of the schools that have issued those degrees.

Schools without accreditation seeking to give degrees do so without the recognition of others. A pastor in Florida was recently hired and quickly asked to step down following an investigation into his credentials. He *had* received degrees, but all of those degrees were from a school that was not accredited. The church could not take seriously the degrees because of the lack of integrity of the institution that distributed those degrees.

At this point you are probably wondering what the point is. Allow me to tie in the introduction to what we are talking about today. My focus today is this: For us to take God's name seriously, we must take God seriously. His name is completely worthy of honor because of the integrity of the One holding that name. Based on the One who holds that name, the Name is worthy of honor. In the same way that the integrity of the school determines

your response to my degree, so our response to the Name ought to be fueled by our worship of the One who holds that name. Do you know God as Savior? Do you know Him as Lord of your life? Do you know Him as your Father and Master? Then that ought to affect the way that we treat His name.

The opposite of a God-centered theology is a ME-centered theology. We have already talked about this in previous devotionals. In this line of thinking, I am at the center of my world and God is there to serve me. That affects everything that we have talked about this week. If I follow that line of thinking, I won't recognize the greatness of His name because it flies in the face of me. I will not be careful carrying His name because I am too concerned with carrying my own name. I certainly will bring down the Name because it brings me up in the process. And then just yesterday we talked about making the most of every opportunity. I will certainly do that, but always in my own interest. That is a Me-centered theology. Have you ever been guilty of a me-centered theology? Sure, we all have. And because we all have, we can quickly see how it affected our great reverence for the name of God. When our minds are consumed with ourselves, we are not concerned with how our actions hurt the witness of the gospel and the church as a whole. Those are sideline details as we live for ourselves. But when ours is a God-centered theology, our lives revolve around God's plan and God's will. Never would we dishonor the One we serve. Never would we carry His name in an unworthy manner. Never would we bring down His name through profane words. Because I know the greatness of God, I know the greatness of the Name, and I want to uphold His Name.

This chapter has been all about the name of God, and living a life worthy of carrying that name. I want to challenge you to go out this week as a missionary for the name of God because that's what you are. Whether you realize it or not, there are those that are watching your walk in order to know what it means to walk for Christ. Carry the name well. God is worthy to be praised!

Connecting with the Commandments
WEEK THREE

Opening Discussion: As you begin the discussion today, talk to your kids about the meaning of their names. Tell the story of how you decided that this would be their name and why it was significant. Also, share how your parents named you and the meaning attached to your name.

Purpose of Activity: As you wrap up that discussion, share that today's "Connecting with the Commandments" time is about how God's name is so special mainly because of who He is. We respect His name because we respect God.

Share this insight from this Week…
One of the stories that the adults heard this week was of a man that wrote a book about the Ten Commandments. This author told a story in his book of a time when he had heard some adults saying some really ugly words and because he was still little, he wasn't sure if those were good words or bad words. So that night, at supper, he decided that he would say one of those bad words and when he did, the look on his daddy's face let him know that he had better not ever say that again!
Why was what he said bad? Well, in the story he tells us that he was using God's name like a bad word. And the Bible teaches us that we are to never use God's name in a bad way. The author who told the story was using God's name to put somebody else down, and that is never how we should use God's name. We should always say His name when we are saying something good.

Favorite Football Team or Favorite Singing Group
Ask your children to talk about their favorite football team or (if they are not into sports) talk about their favorite singing group. Talk about how wearing the jersey of that team, or having a poster of your favorite singer, tells a lot about who you are but it also tells us a lot about your team. When they act really well, people think good things about their team. But when they act really bad, that makes people think that they must have a bad team too.

In the same way, when we use God's name in good ways as we say good things about Him, that says a lot about us just as it says good things about God.

Exodus 20:7
"You shall not take the name of the LORD your God in vain, for the LORD will not hold him guiltless who takes His name in vain."

Explaining the Passage: To "take the name of the Lord your God in vain" means that we use God's name in the wrong way. So let's use God's name in the right way today.

As we seek to use God's name in the right way today, let's come up with ways that we can praise God for who He is and for what He does.

God, you are good because…

God, I love you because…

God, thank you for…

God, one thing that I have learned about you at church is…

When we use God's for anything other than saying good things about Him or using His name as we talk to Him, we're using His name in the wrong way. Sometimes you might hear people use God's name when they're frustrated. When you hear that, pray for that person, that they will understand that God loves them and can help them in their difficult times.

Closing Prayer: God, thank you that we can call on Your name. Thank you for loving us and help us to love You as we use Your name in good ways. Thank you for this time with my family. Amen.

THE MEASURE OF LOVE

CHAPTER FOUR

The Measure of our Trust

ঌ৵

The Measure of our Trust

Daily Scripture Passage:
Genesis 2:2
"By the seventh day God had finished the work he had been doing; so on the seventh day he rested from all his work."

Exodus 20:8-11
"Remember the Sabbath day by keeping it holy. Six days you shall labor and do all your work, but the seventh day is a Sabbath to the LORD your God. On it you shall not do any work, neither you, nor your son or daughter, nor your manservant or maidservant, nor your animals, nor the alien within your gates. For in six days the LORD made the heavens and the earth, the sea, and all that is in them, but he rested on the seventh day. Therefore the LORD blessed the Sabbath day and made it holy."

Thought to Consider: The Purpose of the Sabbath

What an archaic principle to consider a Sabbath day! That might be the response of most everyone in today's secularized culture. Besides, Sunday is the only day I have to get caught up on work. Besides, Sunday is the only day I have to get ahead for the next week. On and on we disregard this law of God as irrelevant and incompatible with our lives in the 21st century. And yet the command of God remains - rest. My goal today is to introduce you to the purpose of the Sabbath. Today's devotional may be a bit longer than most because I want to begin today by addressing a very relevant issue - those who work on Sundays. I pray that you see this command not as one inapplicable to your life, but as an area you need to give careful consideration to in light of the command of God.

As we begin this chapter, I certainly want to recognize that there are positions and duties that now require individuals to work on Sunday. We depend on emergency medical personnel, as well as personnel to maintain power and water facilities, law enforcement and fire fighters. So there are certainly those and other careers which, unfortunately, will require working on Sunday. To those who fall into this category the principle still remains. You need a Sabbath - a day set apart for rest and revival. But because of your work, your day of rest may not be on Sunday as God intended. Hear me out on this next statement - I would be falling short of what God has laid on my heart not to challenge you to seek out a way to adjust your work schedule or even your place of employment so that you can be in corporate worship on Sundays. *But* if that is not possible at this time in your life, then I want to challenge you to realize that regardless of the limitations placed on you by your work, we all need an opportunity to be revived spiritually. I believe that is the heart and purpose of our Sabbath - revival. We will talk about that later in this chapter. Whether that time of revival takes place on Sunday, as God intended, or on another day, the truth remains - you need a time of rest. That means that you may need to discipline yourself on Wednesdays to finish work in time, or make a special request to your boss, so that you can participate in a local church's Wednesday evening services. Many churches offer discipleship type classes on Wednesday nights, or even a preaching service. Whatever the case, to rob yourself of a Sabbath that was God's plan for our lives will harm your everyday life (including your family) and it will greatly hinder your spiritual growth. Again, understanding that your job may keep you from worship on Sundays, I still want to challenge you to seek out an opportunity for corporate worship and fellowship with believers. As we study together this week, consider your commitment to a Sabbath and determine to make this a priority in your life not because it was once a custom of a Bible belt town, but because it is a loving instruction from our Heavenly Father.

The purpose of the Sabbath is found in Exodus 20:8 where we are instructed to keep the Sabbath "holy". As you may know, the word holy literally means "to be set apart". The purpose of this one day is not just slumber, but for one day to be set apart as unto the Lord. Whether sweeping the floor, cooking dinner, washing your car, or a host of other things are allowed on Sundays are trivial issues. The issue is this: "Am I setting aside a day unto the Lord?" It is a mystery why we do not consider this a wonderful gift from God. Our God designed and instructed us to observe a time of rest. Rather than accept this wonderful gift, we bypass it and continue down the path we have created for ourselves. We deem our plans greater than God's.

But what He is saying to you today is this: "I have created You, I know You intimately, and I have provided a time of rest for you. Take it. In fact, I command you to take it." Now that may sound like harsh instruction, but these are loving words from our heavenly Father. My son and daughter would much rather eat chocolate cake and drink sodas for breakfast, lunch, and dinner. But as their father, I have to instruct them in the best way, even

when it sounds harsh or unfair to them. The purpose of the Sabbath is for rest and revival. It is an opportunity to worship the God who created us and has given us the last six days. Besides, are not each of those days a gift from God? As we consider the fourth commandment, I want to challenge you to see it in a new light. It is not a restrictive commandment. It is a command to experience much needed rest and revival each and every week. I want to encourage you to pray for revival this week, and that this revival would especially take place on this Sabbath Sunday.

What were some things growing up that your family was not to do on Sundays?

What is one thing (or a few things) that you just will not do on Sundays?

Do you think that not doing those things is linked to social norms or biblical truth?

I think that many of us have learned over the years certain activities that just were not to be done on Sundays. We may even feel that if we adhere to those instructions, that we are honoring the Sabbath. But the focus of the Sabbath is much more than eliminating certain chores. Again, it is on the fact that it is "holy" - set apart for the Lord. Not doing certain things is fine - if the motive is to set that time apart for the Lord.

How does today's devotional challenge you?

The Measure of our Trust

Daily Scripture Passage: Deuteronomy 5:12-15
"Observe the Sabbath day by keeping it holy, as the LORD your God has commanded you. Six days you shall labor and do all your work, but the seventh day is a Sabbath to the LORD your God. On it you shall not do any work, neither you, nor your son or daughter, nor your manservant or maidservant, nor your ox, your donkey or any of your animals, nor the alien within your gates, so that your manservant and maidservant may rest, as you do. Remember that you were slaves in Egypt and that the LORD your God brought you out of there with a mighty hand and an outstretched arm. Therefore the LORD your God has commanded you to observe the Sabbath day."

Thought to Consider: A Sabbath for your Daily Life

Do you find yourself making it to the weekend and crashing in exhaustion? Has another work week sapped the life out of you once again? We all have experienced this type of exhaustion, so today I want us to take a look at how a Sabbath is a gift from God for relief and rest from our daily lives. Take a look at this recent study by the National Institute for Occupational Safety and Health (NIOSH) which concluded the following:

40% of workers reported their job was very or extremely stressful;

25% view their jobs as the number one stressor in their lives;

75% of employees believe that workers have more on-the-job stress than a generation ago;

29% of workers felt quite a bit or extremely stressed at work;

26 % of workers said they were "often or very often burned out or stressed by their work";

I was watching a program recently that spoke of the company boss taking the employees out to a ridge overlooking the city. He pointed off toward an area

of extremely large homes and told the staff, "You keep working hard like you are and one day I'll have a home right there." You might have expected him to be challenging them to work hard so that *they* might have a home there, but we all know the reality of the workplace. Often your hard work pays for the boss' large home!
Stress affects every aspect of who you are, not only in your work environment, but also in your marriage or family life. It is to this way of life that God says, "rest".

I believe there are those of us who feel a sense of guilt over the idea of resting from our labor. Particularly with men, so often our identity is so attached to our work life that we feel out of place outside of that environment. It is as if we do not know how to act when we're not working. To illustrate this, while our children were still small our family went to the beach with some of our friends. This friend owns a landscaping business where he is constantly digging holes and trenches and working with bulldozer-type equipment. While we were there at the beach we had the idea of digging a hole for the children to play in. Of course, the small hole that we were able to dig on the first day did not suffice. The next day this friend went to the store for one purpose - to purchase a full-size shovel in order to dig a hole so tall that we could not even see them after they walked down into the hole. While we were there we joked about the fact that even on vacation, he could not get away from work and digging. For so many of us we really do have a difficult time just getting away from work!

I pray that we see today that God's Word is not *suggesting* that we rest, but *commanding* that we do it. If God was able to complete His creation in six days and then REST, how do we justify continuing our labor right on through this time designed for our refueling and energizing for another week?

Today's "Thought to Consider" is that we need a Sabbath for our daily life. Tomorrow we will talk about a Sabbath for our spiritual lives, but I want to first of all focus on the very practical side of this commandment. God is instructing us to take a break from the stress of our everyday lives. In my study of this commandment, I found one author who briefly mentioned the fact that the Sabbath provides the benefit of a break from our everyday lives and I was captivated by that thought. God, in His infinite wisdom, saw fit to command us to stop. He is not so impressed with our busyness that He urges us to continue. Rather, He is more interested in our stopping for a moment, just one day out of seven, to remember who He is and to remind ourselves of who we are - children of our Heavenly Father.

You may be thinking that I had you read the same passage today as the previous devotional, but there is a marked difference in today's reading and the similar passage in Exodus. Added to the commandment are these words, "Remember that you were slaves in Egypt and that the Lord your God brought you out of there with a mighty hand and an outstretched arm. Therefore the Lord your God has commanded you to observe the Sabbath day." (NIV)

God was saying this to the people of Israel: "I have it all under control!" He was telling them to stop trying to live life for themselves. If they would have tried to do that while they were in Egypt, they would still be in Egypt! It was only when they turned toward Israel and started walking in faith, even across dry land where a river once was, that they experienced God in control.

I believe this is what God wants us to learn in relation to the Sabbath. It is to be separated - set apart - because God is in control and we are recognizing that fact. We realize that He is our Redeemer and Provider. He is worthy of setting aside this day unto Him. I will not work on in tireless labor believing that any of this is the result of my work. Instead, I am going to stop, knowing that every good gift is from the Father. Regardless of how hard they worked, the Israelites could not have moved one step outside of Egypt without God's provision. They were dependent on God.

Today's challenge is to accept the gift of a Sabbath from your daily life. You need it. It is His gift to you. Don't turn away this wonderful gift that was designed in creation.

Are you stressed? Are you weary from your everyday life? Then take an opportunity this Sabbath to turn your thoughts to Him, demonstrated by your actions. I believe each week that you make this the goal of "the weekend" you will experience new rest and new peace that comes from the Father.

What would be the biggest change you would have to make in order to obey the fourth command?

What benefit(s) do you believe you would experience if you obeyed the fourth commandment on a regular basis?

Your prayer for today...

ಣಜ

The Measure of our Trust

Daily Scripture Passage: Psalm 46:10
Be still, and know that I am God;
I will be exalted among the nations,
I will be exalted in the earth! (NKJV)

Thought to Consider: A Sabbath for your Spiritual Life

The Sabbath is more than just rest from your daily life. It is rest for your spiritual life - a time when you recharge and recommit to the journey of faith towards Christ-likeness. I can remember some of the greatest Sabbath times in my teenage years. Those moments took place at church camp. Church camp for our youth group involved loading up on a bus headed for Cheraw, SC. About the only thing that Cheraw was known for then was a cola bottling plant and good high school football teams. But off in the woods of Cheraw State Park was a camp built by the Civilian Conservation Corps. There our church carried out a church camp each and every year. And there in those woods I had the opportunity to truly get away from all the stuff back home - as wonderful as all that "stuff" was. I can remember times of revival that took place there in that camp. In fact, it was at that camp that I made public the calling that God had placed on my life for the ministry - a calling that I had been praying about for some time. But it was also there that I witnessed many of my friends make commitments for Christ - many for the first time. While there was nothing glamorous about that camp, it did allow youth the opportunity to get away from the distractions all around and to experience revival. It was an opportunity to stop and take inventory on our spiritual lives.

During the summer prior to the writing of this material, the thought that the Sabbath was an opportunity to rest from our daily lives intrigued me. I realized just how easy it is to go through the motions, as good as those might be, week after week and not be growing spiritually. Without a time to stop and take inventory of my spiritual life, I may be headed down a road to spiritual complacency and never realize it. Even church attendance can become so routine that it is no longer reviving you spiritually *if* you are coming into His presence not prepared for and expecting spiritual growth. If that is the case right now in your walk with the Lord, then you need a

Sabbath for your spiritual life. You need an opportunity for revival to take place. That is where we are turning our attention today.

Today I want to speak to the issue of a Sabbath for your spiritual life. The purpose of the Sabbath is to set apart a day unto the Lord. That has already been said quite a few times in this chapter. But beyond simply setting a day aside, I want to challenge you today to set aside a time for *revival* to take place. We cannot manufacture revival. Revival is a gift from God and the result of His people seeking His face in prayer. But I also recognize the fact that revival cannot take place if we never begin that "seeking" and that "praying".

Many of you grew up attending revival services. Some of the services were four days, seven days, or some even fourteen days. In rare cases the services were not even planned, but were the result of God's Spirit moving in the hearts of His people. While on a visit to The Cove: Billy Graham Training Center I walked the lower hallway filled with memoirs of the ministry of Billy Graham. One of the many pictures was of the 1957 New York Revival services, lasting 16 weeks! While I have often heard "You can't schedule revival," I believe this is only partially true. The reason I say partially is because of what I have observed take place as hearts are changed as a result of meetings designed for revival. Through the progression of a time set apart for worship and instruction, we are able to see our sinfulness and our disobedience to God's commands in a way that stirs revival. We all need a time of Sabbath for our spiritual lives.

I have a long history of heart disease in my family. My own father passed away at age 37 from a heart attack. Needless to say, I have concern regarding my own heart health. So several years ago I went to a cardiologist to get a thorough checkup. Connected to a multitude of sensors, I stepped on the treadmill and they began to thoroughly wear me out! Once the treadmill punishment was over, I was to lie on a table immediately, and of all things, hold my breath as they took pictures of my heart. Fortunately, all is well and my heart appears to be in top shape. My point is this - I could have ignored the pleas of my family members to have a check-up, but because I went I now have an accurate picture of my heart's condition and good health. We need to do the same in our spiritual lives - and that is the goal of a Sabbath for your spiritual life. It is a time that you determine to set aside today for a spiritual checkup; a time when you are willing to ask the difficult questions of yourself regarding your commitment to Christ. Then following that time of inspection, be willing to take the steps necessary for real life change.

Let me give you an example. When I was about 15, I attended one of those overnight events for our youth group. You know, the ones that make you feel utterly miserable the next day and that I avoided like the plague once I became a youth minister. Well, at that event the speaker probably said a lot of things, but one thing that he repeated was this: "You have to read your Bible if you are going to grow spiritually." How profound! Now that may sound like an obvious statement, but for me it was a wake-up call. It was a Sabbath moment where I heard God's servant and allowed what he said to challenge my heart. I needed to make a change. It was going to be work, and it is still work today. But I needed to commit to reading God's Word. That was a Sabbath moment because I did not allow all of the distractions of my life to keep me from looking to God. I could have been preoccupied with which girls had shown up that night (and probably was the rest of the night), but instead God allowed me for that moment to hear the Word and then to begin the tough work of applying it.

And so today I ask you, when was the last time that you had a time of Sabbath for your spiritual life? Has there been a time when you allowed yourself to stop and assess your spiritual growth? I want to invite you to do that this week and then be prepared to act on what God calls you to do.

When was the last time that you experienced revival through a Sabbath experience?

What are you praying right now would take place in your life through a Sabbath experience?

How are you going to make this Sunday a Sabbath Experience - a time truly set apart for the Lord?

The Measure of our Trust

Daily Scripture Passage: Exodus 16:11-30 (NKJV)
11 And the LORD spoke to Moses, saying, 12 "I have heard the complaints of the children of Israel. Speak to them, saying, 'At twilight you shall eat meat, and in the morning you shall be filled with bread. And you shall know that I am the LORD your God.'"
27 Now it happened that some of the people went out on the seventh day to gather, but they found none. 28 And the LORD said to Moses, "How long do you refuse to keep My commandments and My laws? 29 See! For the LORD has given you the Sabbath; therefore He gives you on the sixth day bread for two days. Let every man remain in his place; let no man go out of his place on the seventh day." 30 So the people rested on the seventh day."

Thought to Consider: Trusting in His Provision

In the summer of 2006 there were rumors that the warehouse giant Costco might be coming to the nearby mall area. It was going to be an exciting addition because it could fill a large vacated space in the mall and add competition to the market. If you're a warehouse shopper, you've probably discovered that buying in bulk is great for some items, and a bit inconvenient for others. Need a roll of toilet paper? If you are in a warehouse type store, plan to buy enough for a year's supply.

I was recently reading a letter from a missionary in South America. He was so excited because their family had discovered a Sam's or Costco type store miles away where they could finally buy in bulk. Up to that point their only other choice had been the small local markets where items such as sugar and flour were packaged in very small amounts. They could finally buy the mega-packs of food!

For most of us, there are very few times when we can remember wondering from day to day what we were going to eat. While we may not like what's still in the cabinets, with supermarket stores and wholesale clubs like Sam's and Costco, our day to day living is typically filled with abundance.

As we consider our passage for today we see the people of Israel both depending on God's provision, and at the same time we see them concerned with God's provision. There were those within the camp that heard the

instruction and followed it. They gathered only enough food for the day and depended on God for the next day's provision. But then there were those who just could not believe that there would be enough for the next day. I would have to be honest and say that I wonder if I would have been in this camp. As much as I would have wanted to trust the instructions, I imagine my house would have reeked of rotten food the following day.

The instruction was clear. There would be ample provision for five days. On the sixth day there would not only be enough for that day, but ample food for the next day - the Sabbath. It was wholesale club day! There would be no need to collect on the Sabbath because God had already provided ample food for the day.

Do you understand how that principle applies to our lives today? The context of God's command for us to rest is rooted in the fact that He has promised to provide for our needs in six days. On the seventh, we are to stop for rest and revival. That is why I have titled today's devotional, "Trusting in His Provision," because today we need to determine in our hearts that we will trust in His provision, even if it means we deny ourselves a luxury or abundance because of it. Do you trust God? Do you trust Him enough to turn away from work just for this one day so that you can rest and be revived in your walk with Him?

I believe true revival will take place in our hearts when we begin to understand the importance of the Sabbath. I believe when we determine that we will trust God's provision for our lives through six days and rest on the seventh, that we will truly experience revival. We will have a new dependence and submissiveness to God's will and plan for our lives.

As I study this passage of Scripture I find it interesting how many times the people are reminded of the Sabbath. Notice in verse 5 where they are told to gather enough on the sixth day to cover the seventh when there would be no manna or quail. Again in verse 19 they are told to not gather beyond the day's need. Once again in verse 23 they are reminded that the seventh day was the Sabbath. In the case that they have missed the point, in verse 25 they are told to eat it today, because the Sabbath is coming tomorrow. To clarify the previous instruction, in verse 26 Moses expounds on why he told them to eat it

"On the sixth day they are to prepare what they bring in, and that is to be twice as much as they gather on the other days." Ex. 16:5

"Six days you are to gather it, but on the seventh day, the Sabbath, there will not be any." Ex. 16:26

then. But what do we find them doing in verse 27? Here they are out in the field looking for manna and quail. Incredible! My mother would have said, "Clean out your ears so you can hear me!" To this point - in just this one passage - they have been told *five times* what they were to do. But it is in verse 29 that the Lord speaks directly to Moses about the issue once again and there reminds him of the gift of the Sabbath. It is here that God once again reminds Moses of His provision for His people and the clear command to not go out on that seventh day. It is only at this point that it appears the people have received the message.

This is the measure of God's love for us. What God said to Moses was not in harsh condemnation, although that certainly was warranted. God was declaring His provision for His people and the expected obedience to follow.

I believe we need to be reminded once again, much like the Israelites, that God's provision of the Sabbath is for His glory and for our good. (Isn't obedience always for our good?). We need to be reminded that God does not desire to keep us from providing for our families or completing our work by requesting that we set aside one day for Him. Instead He is challenging us to realize that apart from Him we have nothing. He will provide!

ঌ৵

The Measure of our Trust

Daily Scripture Passage: Luke 10:38-42
As Jesus and his disciples were on their way, he came to a village where a woman named Martha opened her home to him. She had a sister called Mary, who sat at the Lord's feet listening to what he said. But Martha was distracted by all the preparations that had to be made. She came to him and asked, "Lord, don't you care that my sister has left me to do the work by myself? Tell her to help me!"

"Martha, Martha," the Lord answered, "you are worried and upset about many things, but only one thing is needed, Mary has chosen what is better, and it will not be taken away from her."

Thought to Consider: A Commitment to Rest

As we enter into this fifth and final devotional for this week, we have the opportunity for a time of commitment related to this week's topic. So with that purpose in mind, the material for today will be shorter than previous days. It will allow you time to focus in on a commitment that God is calling you to make regarding today or any of our previous chapters as well as a focused time of prayer.

As we reflect back on the topic of this week I recognize that there are differing opinions about what is "allowed" on Sundays. I am not interested in establishing a checklist for what we can and cannot do on Sundays, nor do I believe that was God's purpose (see Mark 2:23-28). Instead, we accomplish this command by glorifying Him with our lives through setting apart the Sabbath, holy unto the Lord. So as we set that as our objective, take the time today to seek God's direction in your life regarding a Sabbath rest.

Spend a few minutes in prayer asking God to reveal how you can "set apart" the Sabbath.

Ask God to show you ways to be prepared for this Sabbath Sunday, to worship Him in spirit and truth - not distracted by so many things.

Pray that God will reveal to you ways that you are breaking this commandment and what you need to do for obedience.

My prayer of commitment for today's devotional time:
"Lord, would You send revival like in the time of Hosea where he prayed for a downpour of Your Spirit. Help us to be faithful in serving You and setting aside the Sabbath that You declared as holy. Help us to observe the Sabbath not out of tradition or cultural norms but out of a heart that seeks to honor You above all else. Help us to make serving You our number one priority, over anything or anyone else in our lives. Lord, help us to reveal the measure of our worship by the importance we place on Your day. Lord, we need a passion for You over the multitude of distractions and tasks that are stealing away our focus. Would You burden our hearts for nothing less than loving You, learning You, and living for You? We praise You Lord for who You are. Amen."

Connecting with the Commandments
WEEK FOUR

Opening Discussion: *As you begin today, ask your children what their favorite day of the week is and have them share why that is their favorite day. After they share, offer your favorite day and why that day stands out to you.*

Purpose of Discussion: Today we are going to talk about the fact that God has made one day of the week really special. That special day is Sunday. It's the day that God set aside when He created the world – the day when He rested from all of His work. And from that point forward He has told us that we are to rest and to worship on that day just like He rested. So the reason that we go to church and worship God on Sundays is because this is God's special day, reserved just for Him!

Favorite Things to Do on Sundays: *Because many people are able to be off of work on Sundays, this is often a day for special times. Talk to your kids for a moment about what you like to do on Sundays. Maybe it is your day to take a nap. Maybe it is your day to watch football and just relax. After you share, ask your kids what they like to do on Sunday.*

God asks that we keep HIM at the center of our Sundays.
In the Bible, Sunday is called the Sabbath day. That is just a fancy word for rest or a day that is set apart from the others. Sundays are supposed to be a special day because this is when God commands us to stop our busy lives and take time to be with Him in church and to take a break from the stress of the rest of the week. Believe it or not, God actually designed Sundays for us, so that we would remember Him and that we would also be recharged for another week!

Play a Trust Game
Take a few minutes to play a game intended to test the trust of your kids. Have your child/children put on a blindfold and have a sibling or parent direct them around the room or house. They must depend on the directions of the guide.

Purpose of Activity: Just as you had to trust your guide, so God asks that we trust Him, that six days are enough for accomplishing what we need to do. We demonstrate our trust when we stop our efforts for one day and keep that day reserved for Him.

Closing Challenge: As a family, take a moment to commit to Sunday being God's special day, reserved for Him. Commit to trusting that God will allow you to accomplish enough in 6 days so that Sundays will remain His day!

THE MEASURE OF LOVE

CHAPTER FIVE

The Measure of Honor

ꕥ

The Measure of Honor

Daily Scripture Passage: Exodus 20:12
"Honor your father and your mother, so that you may live long in the land the LORD your God is giving you."

Thought to Consider: Being Honorable Parents

I want to congratulate you on your continued study of the Ten Commandments. In 1st Timothy, Paul challenged Timothy to demonstrate diligence and persistence in his walk with Christ and that is what you are demonstrating by your faithfulness to this devotional time. I pray that the Holy Spirit has moved in your heart as you have invested in this time. Many in our congregation from several years ago had already shared by this point how this series had been a blessing and how God had used it to teach and challenge them. I pray the same is true for you. That alone is confirmation enough for the time invested in this series.

In this chapter, we come to the dividing line of the Ten Commandments. While the first four commandments deal with our relationship to God, the latter six deal with our relationship with people and how we are to live as God's children. Beginning this division is the command to honor your parents. The principle behind this command is the same as the principle behind the Ten Commandments as a whole - our obedience is motivated by the Measure of our Love. The command for obedience is the result of and Measure of God's Love.

As we come to this command there is one clear fact: our parenting is not perfect (nor are our children perfect). I have tried to teach truth through these devotionals and I believe I can confidently assert the following fact: none of us have perfected parenting nor raised perfect children. So as we come to this command we are going to look at it from both sides, because regardless of our desires - neither parents nor children will walk in perfection in regards to this command this side of glory.

In his book *Do We Still Need the Ten Commandments?*, John Timmerman addresses the issue of being an honorable parent, and being a child who honors. Have you considered the first? Maybe your focus has been on the latter, but if we are to assume the respect of our children, we need to be parents that are honorable. The first task of being a parent worthy of honor is loving our children. We must remember that this is the context of God's commands, and as such, should be the context of our obedience to the fifth command. We must obey and expect obedience to this command in love. As Timmerman states, "Parents who represent God's authority will love their children for *who they are*, rather than *what they might do*." Because of that love I do not disregard rules and limitations. Rather, the rules and guidelines for my children are based on my love for them. I do not want them to disobey because I believe that the ultimate consequences for that behavior are greater than the punishment they must endure in correction. To be an honorable parent, I must love my children.

Proverbs 6:20 says, "My son, keep your father's commands, and do not forsake your mother's teaching." As a parent worthy of honor, I must direct my children. Timmerman says, "A lack of directing, or letting a child do anything he or she pleases, may be a sign of lack of love or, at best, a sadly misdirected love." I must love my child by directing them in the way of life, particularly in a lifestyle of faith!

Lastly, to be a parent worthy of honor, I must be willing to nurture my children. This goes beyond discipline. It involves instruction in right living. Now this might come at a time when my child has chosen the wrong path, but I must always be willing to stop and teach.

Upward basketball has become an incredibly successful basketball ministry because of its focus on teaching biblical truths in the context of sports. One of the things that I love about the format of the basketball ministry is that teaching is always more important than the game. If the game needs to be stopped in order to teach a group of small children why fouling is wrong, then that is what is done. Teaching is always more important than the score or who wins.

The lesson from *Upward* basketball applies well to nurturing children. In my disgust over my child's disobedience, discipline is often my first thought. But to be parents worthy of honor, our first thought ought to be teaching and training so that they do not choose this path again. Discipline may be a grand motivator in this process, but it should never the sole teacher.

I want to be a parent worthy of honor. I pray you do as well. But if you gather anything from today's devotional, I pray that you understand that the fifth commandment is as much about being honorable as a parent as it is about being honored as a parent.

What are some ways that you could be a more honorable parent?

How were your parents honorable? Dishonorable?

Spend a few minutes in prayer asking God to help you to be honorable in the way that you raise your children.

❧

The Measure of Honor

Daily Scripture Passage: Hebrews 13:7 NLT
Remember your leaders who taught you the word of God. Think of all the good that has come from their lives, and follow the example of their faith.

Thought to Consider: Being Children Who Honor

In the immediate application of this passage, we come to a commandment that we do not have to apply at all stages of our lives. As D. James Kennedy points out in his book, *Why the Ten Commandments Matter*, "It is the only commandment you do not have to keep all of your life. In fact, you can't keep it after your parents have died because it's too late. If your parents are still living, the time to honor them is now." We are going to take a look at the broader application of this commandment later in this chapter, but in its immediate application, the time for obedience to this commandment is now. It reminds us to be cautious about living for tomorrow. Before long tomorrow will pass and we will realize that we never lived in the joy of today. Our parents will grow old and our lives will be filled with regrets.

In our passage for today we read a clear instruction from the writer of Hebrews, "Remember your leaders, who spoke the word of God to you. Consider the outcome of their way of life and imitate their faith."

If we are to be children who honor, then we need to be willing to follow the example of those that have taught us the Word of God. I am grateful for my upbringing in the church. Because of my parents' dedication to the Lord, we were always in worship on Sundays. I had the opportunity to grow up in a youth ministry where I could explore God's call on my life and then surrender to that calling.

As a youth, I had to decide that I would respect the wishes of my mother and be in church. I had to learn to "imitate" or follow her example of faith. Now there were certainly times when I would have rather remained in the bed, but through her example of faith, I chose to be a child who honored. (Her discipline was motivation as well, as it should have been!)

What a powerful statement this verse makes! "Consider the outcome of their faith!" In other words, in all your supposed wisdom as a teenager or college age individual, did you ever think to stop and look at your parents' lives and realize they might have known what they were talking about from time to time?

If we are going to apply this passage to our lives, then I encourage you today to consider what it is about your parents' life that is worth imitating. Were they always faithful in church attendance? Was prayer central to their lives? Did they realize their failures and confess them? Whatever the case, I know in my own life there are qualities that I learned to emulate. But at the same time, there are those even within our own congregation whose parents did not display these noble qualities. Honor your parents, but do so by not honoring and repeating those ignoble qualities, but by learning from their mistakes and rising above their failures.

What is one quality that you remember about your parents that you wish you could "imitate" as Hebrews 13:7 instructs us?

What is a quality that your children are learning from you, good or bad?

What quality do you want your children to see in you as they seek to honor you?

The Measure of Honor

Daily Scripture Passage: Ephesians 6:1-4 NKJV
Children, obey your parents in the Lord, for this is right. "Honor your father and mother," which is the first commandment with promise: "that it may be well with you and you may live long on the earth."
And you, fathers, do not provoke your children to wrath, but bring them up in the training and admonition of the Lord.

Thought to Consider: Too Sophisticated for Love

Preparing for this chapter's material took on new meaning as I am a parent now of elementary age children, as hard as that is for me to believe. This commandment now applies to me in two ways, not only as a son, but now as a parent. I need to be a parent worthy of honor, as we spoke of on day one. But for many of us, we are still sons and daughters of parents still with us. And that's where I want to turn our focus today.

Do you remember when hugging mom or dad stopped being cool? Do you remember when it embarrassed you for them to make a big deal out of goodbyes before school or church trips? There comes that point in a young kid's life where it is not as cool to get that hug from mom or dad. Then there comes that time when we just become "too sophisticated" for all that hugging stuff. Maybe you remember that time in your own life, or you might have been the wonderful exception that never went through this odd stage. At the same time there may be those of you today who have never outgrown that "too sophisticated" stage of life and to this day rarely express your love for your parents.

I was reading a story this week about a pastor who had two little boys. When his boy was about elementary age he asked him one time, "Are you proud of who your daddy is (a pastor)?" His son did not reply. It was like a knife cutting through his heart. In that moment he realized that it wasn't popular for him to go to school and say that his daddy was the preacher of the church. He didn't like being the subject of the illustrations used in the pulpit. So rather than say something mean that day, he just didn't reply. For many years that thought remained in the father's mind. Are my kids still embarrassed of me? Do they resent what their father does?

Many years later Pastor Mehl was celebrating his anniversary at his church and the staff arranged a special service. The special guest speaker was a mystery even to the day of the service. Pastor Mehl and his wife were escorted to the front pew to be seated. Then the associate pastor stood and announced that today there would be a special guest speaker...Ron Mehl. Pastor Mehl was a bit taken back by this. He had not prepared. How could the staff do this to him? The associate pastor continued, "Ron Mehl...Jr."

At that announcement Pastor Mehl's son, Ron Jr. stepped up to the mic. Now a college student, he had never spoken before the large crowd. He told of a time when his father had asked him whether he was proud of being a Mehl. He said, "Well, you know how kids are...they want their dad to be pro basketball player or a rocket scientist. But at that time I didn't really know what being a pastor was or what a pastor did. I didn't tell him I was embarrassed, but...I couldn't look at him and tell him I wasn't." Ron Jr. went on to describe what it was like growing up as a pastor's kid and then said the most important words of his father's life. Ron Jr said, "I want to say that I couldn't be any more proud of my parents than I am, and I know that goes for my brother as well. I wouldn't want them to do anything else than to pastor this church. Thanks for loving us and making us proud to be your sons. We love you, Mom and Dad."

As I sat in my office and read that story I was holding back the tears because I know our family will have to walk that same path with pastor's kids. I want to be a parent worthy of honor and I want my son and daughter to be proud of what their dad does in serving the Lord. But I also fear that day when they, like Ron Jr., will appear too sophisticated for love. Fortunately, Ron Jr. came full circle in his love and respect for his dad. He truly honors his father and mother.

Not many of you are pastor's kids, but the application is the same. If you would have been asked many years ago whether you were proud to be a son/daughter of your parents, what would you have said? I understand that some parents did not act in honor as we spoke of on day one, but for many of us, we were raised in wonderful homes. And yet we still find ourselves all too often "too sophisticated" for love.

I ask you this morning, has your life come full circle like Ron Jr.'s, or are you still "too sophisticated" for love? Whether your parents are still living today or not, honor a parent this week. Tell another mom or dad that they're doing a great job and love on them. But for those of you whose parents are still living today, isn't it time to let them know you love them? Let's show our parents this week we aren't too sophisticated for love.

What is one of the greatest memories that you have of your parents?

Has there been a time in your life when you felt "too sophisticated for love"?

Have you been to sophisticated to love on your own children or grandchildren? How so?

Let's get rid of this idea of being too sophisticated to just let those we love know that we love them and to hug their neck. It might be the first hug you've given your parent since you were a child, but it's time. They need to know you love them. Honor them this week.

If you do not have a parent still living, then honor another parent this week. Don't just read that as a kind suggestion - really do it. Stop and think right now, how can I honor a parent today or in the next few days? (As we first went through this material in our own church and came to this section, my wife and I received a wonderful and encouraging note from a member of our church. It was encouraging to hear those words from someone who had taken notice of our children and family!)

Honor your father and mother, so that you may live long in the land the Lord your God is giving you!

The Measure of Honor

Daily Scripture Passage: John 14:15
"If you love Me, keep My commandments."
John 15:10
If you keep My commandments, you will abide in My love, just as I have kept My Father's commandments and abide in His love.

Thought to Consider: Abiding in His Love

With so many individuals reading this devotional series, there is bound to be an individual or two who come to this commandment and scoff at the idea of honoring their parents. We touched on that idea briefly in the last devotional. Your parents may have been absent from the home more than they were there for you. Your parents may have ruled with a harsh discipline that often crossed the line. One of your parents may have treated you in a way that was improper and unfitting of the ones who were supposed to raise you in love. When you come to the commandment to honor your parents, you turn your back and say, "But God knows what I endured!"

There are those times when we can say, "I understand," but this is not one of those times for me. Although my father died when I was just nine years old, I was raised in a stable home where my mother loved us and cared for us unconditionally. But that is not the case in all homes. In far too many homes there is verbal, physical, and even sexual abuse and the scars that accompany that pain run deep. It is to those of you who have endured such a life that I say today, "Abide in His love".

In John 15:10, we are told that as we obey his commands we literally abide in His love. Other translations render it "remain in his love". That is a wonderful promise. You see, regardless of the difficulties of life that we have endured, the command remains. We must honor our parents. They may not be worthy of honor, but the responsibility on our part remains. As we seek to honor our parents, we can abide in His love. The word abide carries the meaning of "dwelling or standing in the presence of". When I imagine the picture of "abiding in His love," I picture a child crawling into the lap of a loving father for comfort and protection. For the individual who has endured a difficult childhood and whose view of their parent is scarred, this is an incredible image.

It is in that context that we face the inevitable truth of this passage - we must honor our parents even when they have acted dishonorably to us. How will you do it? By abiding in *His* love. You are not honoring them based on *their* love, however absent this might have been, but you are honoring them because you are abiding in *His* love.

This line of thinking may be completely new to you - to consider that you might have to honor that dishonorable parent. Taking the next step of honoring your parent may have to be small at first. It may begin with a simple card saying you were thinking about them. From that step you may need to sit down face to face with your mother or father (or both) and openly talk about your childhood with the intent of honoring them according to God's command. If you take this step of a face to face discussion, it is going to be incredibly difficult to not allow hatred and built up anger to surface. For that reason, you need to ask for those in a small group Bible study class or circle of friends to pray for you as you take this step - that you take it in God's strength alone. In fact, there are those of you who are reading this devotional today and you like myself have never had to deal with a harsh or abusive parent. Will you join with me in praying for those whose backgrounds were not as pleasant as our own?

I want to challenge those of you that this devotional speaks to - that you begin today to understand that you abide in His love as you seek to follow the commands. Begin to lean on His love as you seek be a faithful servant of God in even the most difficult parts of your life.

Today, as you consider this command there may be emotional scars with which you have not dealt. Can I encourage you to deal with those scars? Whether it is with a pastor or with a Christian counselor, you need to allow God's healing to take place in your life. No doubt those memories have affected not only your life, but all of those within your family today. Allow God to heal you in some of these areas as you journey through this chapter's commandment.

As we follow the Ten Commandments we abide in His love. What a wonderful promise of Scripture! May we be faithful in living out each of the commands, regardless of the difficult road it may take us down, as the Measure of our Love for Him.

God, today I want to pray for ___________________________ . I think they might have endured a difficult childhood and need my prayers today.

Today you may realize the wonderful blessing of your own childhood in that you did not have to experience any of the great trials that some endure. Use that as a catalyst for blessing those who were instrumental in that wonderful upbringing. If your parents are no longer living, then talk to siblings or close friends about that blessing.

For those that are reading this today and it all hits home, I am praying for you. I want you to take a few minutes now to write down some steps based on today's devotional and Scripture that you are going to take to deal with those difficult issues from your past.

The Measure of Honor

Daily Scripture Passage: 1 Timothy 2:1-2
"I urge, then, first of all, that requests, prayers, intercession and thanksgiving be made for everyone—for kings and all those in authority, that we may live peaceful and quiet lives in all godliness and holiness."

Thought to Consider: The Duty to Pray and Give Thanks for Superiors

In the *Larger Catechism of the Westminister Assembly* we read, "the general scope of the Fifth Commandment is the performance of those duties which we mutually owe in our several relations, as inferiors, superiors, or equals." What the Westminster Catechism is establishing is that the fifth commandment covers a broader scope than just our parents. It also speaks to all of those in authority over us. This is made clear elsewhere in Scripture where we are commanded to honor superiors (Lev. 19:32, 1 Tim. 2:1-2, Heb. 13:7, Eph. 6:1-2).

During this chapter, we have focused our attention on the parent-child relationship as is clear in this command. We even talked about this commandment being one that you only are bound to while your parents are alive. But I believe we can understand from this command, as is clearly illustrated by the Westminister Catechism, that the principle certainly applies beyond the scope of our own parents.

Leviticus 19:32 says, "Rise in the presence of the aged, show respect for the elderly and revere your God. I am the Lord your God." Now there certainly are ceremonial principles all throughout the book of Leviticus that the blood of Jesus Christ has freed us from, but He did not come to fulfill any moral law. The command remains, we must honor our parents, and as this passage suggests, to honor those older than us as well.

I can remember when my grandfather was slowly dying. All of our family rallied around my grandmother to help her care for him as he fought a slow death of cancer. At times he hardly acted like himself, but our love for him caused us to always be there for him. I can remember the night that he died. I sat in the room where his body remained and thought, "What a man! He lived a great life and he loved us so much." I can remember having a great deal of

sorrow, but also pride as I thought about who my grandfather was. Without a doubt we honored his life, even in his dying days.

Our passage in 1 Timothy for today reminds me that if I am to live a godly life in all honesty, then my character and respect must carry beyond the walls of my home. I cannot be one person to my parent and to my children, and then act completely different once I leave those walls.

Once again I remember the words of my friend's mother as he would go out for an evening with friends. I spoke of this in a previous chapter. She would simply say, "Remember who you are!" Remembering who he was did not just apply at home. It especially applied out in the community where their name was known.

The same principle carries across to all of our respect for superiors. Who we are at home only enhances who we will be out in the community.

For those with young children...

How have your children demonstrated what they have learned at home out in the community?

What is one area that you need to work on with your children?

For everyone...

As this commandment applies to all superiors, how can you honor someone this week?

Connecting with the Commandments
WEEK FIVE

Opening Activity: *Share with your children a time when you really felt honored by them. Think of a time when your children did something really nice for you and it made you feel so good. Also, think of some way that you express or expressed love for your parents. What was a fun thing that you did when you were younger that really impressed your parents?*

Today we are talking about "honoring your parents" and you can be sure that this is one of our favorite commandments. We know that this is something that you hear us demanding all of the time – "Listen to what I'm saying!" So today, let's talk about *why* the Bible commands us to respect our parents. Remember, we had parents too and we had to respect our parents just like you do, so let's look together at *why* the Bible tells us to do this.

The Measure of Love
The name of the book that we have been studying is called "The Measure of Love" and what this book is teaching us is that God gives us rules because He loves us. He does not want us to get hurt by bad choices, so He makes rules that help us to know what is right and wrong.
In the same way, that's why God gives you people like parents and teachers. As your parents, we are here to help you learn how to make wise choices, and rules are a part of that learning process, and those rules actually reveal our love.
Egypt Illustration: In January 2011, Egypt (a country at the top of Africa) had a lot of really bad things happening in it. People were mad at the government and wanted change. Well, as the people got mad, the police eventually had to get out of the way to keep from getting hurt. Do you know what happened when the police left? The situation got worse! The angry people started stealing and destroying things. Once the rule enforcers were gone, the people made really bad choices.
Point of Illustration: Just like people started making bad choices once the police were gone, so we would make bad choices if God didn't give us people all around us who are teaching us what it means to live a life that pleases God. So parents are one way that God teaches us how to live like He wants us to live. They help keep us from bad choices – that's how much they love us and that's how much we, as your parents, love you!
Close in Prayer Together – ask God to help you love each other!

THE MEASURE OF LOVE

CHAPTER SIX

The Measure of our Forgiveness

The Measure of our Forgiveness

Daily Scripture Passage: Exodus 20:13
"You shall not murder."
Matthew 5:21-22
"You have heard that it was said to the people long ago, 'Do not murder, and anyone who murders will be subject to judgment.' But I tell you that anyone who is angry with his brother[1] *will be subject to judgment. Again, anyone who says to his brother, 'Raca,' is answerable to the Sanhedrin. But anyone who says, 'You fool!' will be in danger of the fire of hell."*

Thought to Consider: Anger Toward our Brothers

I want to congratulate you again for your commitment to this devotional time. You have been diligent in these matters and I pray that you are seeing the progress! We are now over half-way through our study of the Ten Commandments. Thank you for your perseverance!

In this chapter, we are going to be dealing with the sixth commandment - You shall not murder. I was reading this past week that within every family tree there is a murderer. That statement came as quite a shock to me. I am not familiar with a murderer in my family tree. But I read on and understood. Consider Cain in chapter 4 of Genesis. No, to the best of my knowledge my direct lineage does not contain a murderer, but far back in all of our genealogy is Cain, the first murderer.

Week after week during the initial launch of this material I heard comments on the way this study of the Ten Commandments helped that initial congregation studying this material understand and begin to apply God's law in their lives. But for many of us, we come to this sixth command wondering about its application to our lives. You may say, "I have been angered at times, but never to the point of wanting to permanently harm someone, and by no means murder them." For most of us, that is far from our minds. But before we skip on to the seventh command ignoring the principle of the sixth, let us remind ourselves how Jesus interpreted this command, and then how we see this command interpreted elsewhere in the New Testament.

In Matthew 5:21-22 we see Jesus raising the bar, not with new laws, but with a correct understanding of the basis of the law. He went back to the purpose

In Matthew 5:21-22 we see Jesus raising the bar, not with new laws, but with a correct understanding of the basis of the law.

behind the law. The Pharisees and religious leaders were convinced that their adherence to the law was sufficient obedience, but Jesus challenged their heartless obedience. He said, "I say to you, whoever is angry with his brother without a cause shall be in danger of the judgment." What Jesus was challenging them to see that day was the root of murder. Rarely does murder take place without anger as the beginning point. So with that in mind, let's go to the root of this command by asking the question of what is the beginning point for me that leads to breaking one of God's commands? If we can identify that step of disobedience, then we will better follow God's commands. If I know that hatred leads me down a slippery slope of sin, then I need to address my hatred from the start. If I know that viewing inappropriate television programs leads to lust and down the slippery slope toward adultery, then I need to address my viewing habits from the start. Jesus is teaching us an incredible principle in this passage in Matthew 5. He is saying, "Don't get to the point of utter ruin. Recognize the signs of sin now before you make a total mess of your life." Jesus was challenging the religious leaders to understand that hatred was the root of murder.

For that reason, much of what we are going to be talking about in this chapter will be in reference to hatred and anger because truly those are the root of murder. Is there anger or hatred in your heart toward any individual? Do you hold a grudge towards an action that someone took against you? However justified that anger or hatred might be, it is now your responsibility to forgive, lest you face the judgment.

In this chapter we will be talking about the Measure of Forgiveness. How open are you to forgiving those around you? Who do you need to forgive today?

I want to again recommend Bill Bright's book "*Written by the Hand of God*". I know I have mentioned it in previous chapters because I have found it to be a reliable and easy to understand resource for my own study of the Ten Commandments. In his book, he talks about the different acts that are murder and those that are not. Within that list is an interesting section on killing animals. Now I didn't want to spend a whole day on this topic, but I did think that it was interesting and I thought some of the men reading this material would enjoy this section. For Bill Bright, there actually was a time when he was convinced by another believer that killing an animal was wrong. Let's take a moment to deal with that issue and we will also deal with the issue of drawing the line between killing and murder.

Bill Bright says, "Not all killing is murder. But the narrow scope of the sixth command focuses on the taking of an 'innocent' human life by another human, often with premeditation. According to the great biblical scholar Charles Ryrie, the word 'kill' is used 49 times in the Old Testament. In each case, the word in the original Hebrew language means 'to murder with premeditation.'"

Based on that understanding of the sixth command, premeditation is the distinction for classifying a killing as murder. Within that would fall murdering another human in anger or for revenge, or even taking the life of the unborn. Therefore, according to that definition, capital punishment, acts of war, and self-defense are not excluded by the sixth commandment. In fact, all of these are seen as acceptable practices elsewhere in the Bible.

Well what about animals? Doesn't the command to not kill also include the killing of animals? Remember, there was another believer who actually tried to convince Bill Bright of this fact. But in Genesis 9:3 God says to Noah, "every moving thing that is alive shall be food for you". In 1 Timothy 4, a passage that we read just a few weeks ago in Sunday School, we read about the instruction that every creature is permissible for food as long as it is received with thanksgiving. So this command certainly does not exclude killing animals.

So don't worry guys - no need to pack away the camo and deer stands - you're within God's law when you head out to the woods with the aim of bringing home meat to fill the freezer - - Just remember that God is never more proud of you than when you share!!

ᘛ

The Measure of our Forgiveness

Daily Scripture Passage: 1 John 3:11-15
"For this is the message that you heard from the beginning, that we should love one another, not as Cain who was of the wicked one and murdered his brother. And why did he murder him? Because his works were evil and his brother's righteous.
Do not marvel, my brethren, if the world hates you. We know that we have passed from death to life, because we love the brethren. He who does not love his brother abides in death. Whoever hates his brother is a murderer, and you know that no murderer has eternal life abiding in him." NKJV

Thought to Consider: Forgiving even when it is not earned.

One of the interesting things that I notice about our passage for today is that the focus is never on the acts of the other person. The focus is completely on us. I cannot deny the enormity of that responsibility - that regardless of the actions of another human being, I have the responsibility of forgiveness.

In the first week of October 2006, a horrific event took place when Charles Carl Roberts IV entered an Amish school and began to kill and wound a group of girls from the school. It has since been discovered that the senseless act of violence was linked to the death of his first daughter, who died shortly after birth, as well as abuse that took place during Roberts' childhood. As one reporter cited, Roberts was "acting out of revenge for something that happened 20 years ago". From the example of Roberts' words and actions, we see the importance of forgiveness and the power of hatred within one's life. Hatred can certainly lead to murder, and in the community of Lancaster, Pennsylvania, they are experiencing the ugly truth of that fact. When I read the account of that horrific day, I am angered. The coward that committed those acts turned the gun on himself rather than face the punishment that was due him. While that is my response to this senseless act of violence, what I want you to see today is the response of the people of that community.

The grandfather of two sisters killed by the gunman spoke to WGAL-TV, the NBC affiliate in Lancaster. He was asked by a reporter, "Is there anger towards the gunman's family?" "No," said the grandfather. The reporter then asked, "Have you forgiven?" To which the grandfather said, "In my heart, yes." Shocked by his answer, "How is that possible?" He simply replied, "Through God's help."

It touches my heart to hear those words from that grandfather because he truly understands the principle Jesus taught in Matthew 5, and also the passage we read today in 1 John 3. There is no hatred or anger in his heart. He has already forgiven a murderer.

In the midst of this tragedy, listen to the words of another: "It will provide an example to talk to their children about why violence is bad and why violence is sinful," says Donald Kraybill, a religious scholar at Elizabethtown College in Lancaster. Another goes on to say, "We can tell people about Christ and actually show you in our walk that we forgive, not just say it, but in our walk of life," she says.

"You have heard this message from the beginning: we should love one another." For the members of that Pennsylvania town, they have decided that this truth even applies to the one who has taken the lives of their loved ones. This morning as I write this devotional, I am challenged by their act of forgiveness, but also intrigued. How can they do it? How do they have the strength to demonstrate that level of faith?

Lord, I want to experience the freedom of forgiveness. I do not want to be bound by the actions of others. Instead I want to daily walk in your grace and offer the same forgiveness that you have given me. Lord, help me to actually show others about you in the way that I walk so that when I mention your name they already know that I trust solely in you. Lord, we pray for the families that are now experiencing an immeasurable amount of grief over the loss of their loved ones. Help us to learn from their example of forgiveness by loving our brothers. Amen.

(Source for Material: http://www.msnbc.com - "Amish display the true meaning of forgiveness" 10-4-06)

The material below is a supplement to Day One. If you are short on time, go ahead and move to Day Two in our study. As time allows later in the week, you can return to this section in order to get an extended explanation and study of the topic of anger.

Supplement to Day One

Understanding the Root of our Anger

In our first day of studying the commandment against murder, the material may have evoked a number of different emotions within you. You may have played out the scenario in your mind, considering how you would have reacted in that situation. You may have scoffed at the quick offer of forgiveness, thinking more of revenge than compassion. So as we begin this week together, let's consider for a moment the root of our anger. What leads to that feeling of intense desire to get even and inflict harm on others (both verbally and physically)?

Gary Chapman is an author and speaker, well-known for his book entitled "The Five Love Languages". Recently, however, he has taken up the issue of anger. In his book entitled, "Anger: Handling a Powerful Emotion in a Healthy Way" Chapman addresses this issue in great detail, all for the purpose of helping the believer to be free from the stranglehold of that powerful emotion.

Interestingly, as Chapman begins discussing the root of anger, he actually attributes this to God. Now before you get angry at the simple suggestion, listen to his thinking. He suggests that anger is rooted in holiness. God's holiness compels Him to act when there is evil. In the same way, as we are angered, it is usually in response to a feeling of being wronged and unappreciated. We witness someone doing something wrong, the opposite of holiness, and we react wanting to correct that situation. However, the aspect of God's character that we so often miss is that He is a God of holiness *and* love. So as God is angered by wickedness, His love leads Him to respond very differently than we as sinful men will respond. Rather than retaliate, God offers the chance again and again for redemption, far longer than any of us would be willing to offer.

So as we realize that anger is rooted in our God-created desire for right in our world, we can agree that the emotion by itself is not wrong. However, what is often *very* wrong is our reaction to the emotion of anger. Though our anger is rooted in our desire for right in the world, regardless of whether that perspective is actually founded in truth, we often fail to apply a second aspect of God's character which is love. God *is* holy and His holiness demands justice, but God *is* love, which defines His reaction to wrong. So God reacts to His anger towards wickedness through the vehicle of His love, demonstrated in the cross of Jesus Christ.

Knowing then that anger can be expressed through the vehicle of love, we now acknowledge that we have much to learn. Our world, our jobs, and even our families have the potential of stirring up all levels of anger. That fact is unavoidable. What *is* avoidable though is a wrong expression of our anger in lashing out at those around us in order for our idea of right to be restored. We all ought to be grateful that God did not lash out at us with that same harsh attitude of enforcement of His justice for we all deserve the punishment of His wrath. Instead, realizing the presence of evil, God responded in love and our relationship was restored with God rather than severed.

So following the example of Christ, our anger ought to lead us into action to restore our relationships rather than sever them. Our viewpoint of wrong and injustice should never lead us to amplify the division within family and friendships. As Chapman states, "…I believe that human anger is designed by God to motivate us to take constructive action in the face of wrongdoing or when facing injustice."

Anger is a motivator, but our expression of that motivation must not be in trying to manipulate or control others. Typically those prone to anger are also prone to manipulating and controlling, but that's not what the God-given emotion of anger should propel us to do. Instead, the emotion of anger should stir in us the desire to do whatever is necessary to make right the relationship that is being affected by that anger. Rather than control, we choose love and respect. Rather than manipulation, we choose serving and honoring.

Anger *is* a component of our makeup, but anger is never a license to sin against others and against God. It is an emotion that stirs us into action, but never as permission to hurt others. You may need to take some very practical steps in addressing your anger. That begins with acknowledging that your anger is controlling both you and those around you. Secondly, you must take immediate steps towards restraining your anger. This may be through removing yourself from the situation briefly or withholding a response until you have "cooled off". Third, consider God's responses within Scripture to challenges He faced and respond with that same love. Finally, turn your anger into constructive actions rather than destructive ones. As you continue studying this week, pray for victory in the expression of your anger.

The Measure of our Forgiveness

Daily Scripture Passage: Ephesians 4:2-3
[2] *with all lowliness and gentleness, with longsuffering, bearing with one another in love,* [3] *endeavoring to keep the unity of the Spirit in the bond of peace.*

Thought to Consider: The Source of our Anger

In the supplement to Day One, the issue of anger was discussed in detail, particularly in relation to the root of anger. As you have time, I encourage you to go back and read that material. This week, we are recognizing that if we hold a grudge or anger against anyone, we are murderers in our hearts. That is a strong accusation but it is true. Today, I want to return to some of what we discussed in the supplemental material, and in so doing I do not want to simply point the finger at our guilt. Instead, I want to help you (and myself) recognize the source of anger in our lives. We all have different buttons that people or situations push that trigger our anger (some quicker than others). So we could all benefit from identifying the source of our anger.

What are some of your "pet peeves"? You know, those things that seem to happen all the time and they just irritate you to no end. If I mention driving, there are probably a lot of those pet peeves that come to mind. I cannot stand the slow driver who stays in the fast lane on the interstate. I cannot stand someone who "makes a career" out of turning into their driveway or street, or getting behind someone that seems to be doing a "tour of homes". Those are pet peeves - things that bother me. Those are easily recognizable and rather easy to stop. Those are not the issues that I want to address today. What I want to talk about instead is the anger that is directed at those around you, most importantly - your family. But before you begin creating a list of triggers caused by family members, let's spend time talking about ourselves.

Your Speech
Are your words seasoned with salt, or covered with flaming hot sauce? The Bible says that our tongue can be as piercing as a sword (Prov. 12:18). Do you often find yourself making others mad? Then consider your tongue. Are your words like the first portion of Prov. 12:18 - "piercing like a sword," or are they like the latter, "the tongue of the wise brings healing"? Seek to bring healing with your words, not destruction. Try that today and see the result!

Your Actions
As is the case with most people, I do not like conflict. In fact, I do my best to stay out of conflict. Fortunately, my own marriage seldom experiences conflict. But in those times of conflict, how I react greatly determines the duration of that conflict. I am sure you have learned this first hand. If I react in a constructive way, the problem can often be resolved quickly. But if I react negatively, the problem only grows. My actions greatly affect anger. The Bible says, "So then, my beloved brethren, let every man be swift to hear, slow to speak, slow to wrath;" James 1:19

If we are going to deal with anger, especially among family members, we must be willing to communicate with one another - even in the face of conflict. So, men/women, the "silent treatment" is not a biblical alternative.

If I am going to keep my life free of anger, then I must be willing to bear with one another. In Ephesians 4:2-3 we read, "with all lowliness and gentleness, with longsuffering, bearing with one another in love, endeavoring to keep the unity of the Spirit in the bond of peace." My actions will demonstrate my desire to be free from anger when I am willing to bear with you in the spirit of love, even in the face of conflict. The word "bear" in Eph. 4:2 carries the idea of "enduring or suffering with". Even in the face of difficult times, I must be willing to endure those times right alongside you. What a challenge that is for us - especially if you do not like conflict!

Look for the source of your anger - in your speech and in your actions - and don't let the devil get a foothold in your life in these areas. Open your eyes today and this week to those areas and allow God to stretch you and grow you in those areas of your life.

How am I allowing anger to control my life and the lives of those around me?

What steps can I take today to turn my anger into positive actions?

What would others say about my use of anger?

What can I do today to make situations right where I have wronged others?

The Measure of our Forgiveness

Daily Scripture Passage: Selected Passages in Today's Study
Thought to Consider: The Duties Required by the Sixth Commandment

Throughout my teenage years I learned that not doing certain things definitely strengthened my faith. Although I cannot say I made it through the teenage years sinless by any means, there were certain things that I stayed away from, namely alcohol. I sort of prided myself over the fact that I abstained from alcohol. But as I grew older and began to look back over those teenage years I realized one glaring problem with that stand - I never replaced that stance against a negative influence with the influence of many positives. By that I mean, I became good at saying no to certain things but I was not saying yes to the alternative - studying God's Word, growing in my faith, becoming more like Christ daily. I had become a lazy Christian, satisfied with only a small victory in my journey of faith. Today I want to challenge you, as I challenge myself, to not only say no to hatred and murder, but to also say yes to the alternative - the duties required by the sixth command.

In Ernest Reisenger's book "Whatever Happened to the Ten Commandments", he lists the duties required by the sixth commandment. I want to take time today to look at a few of those requirements and then allow the Holy Spirit to teach us and apply these duties as needed.

The duty to preserve our own life.
"So husbands ought to love their own wives as their own bodies; he who loves his wife loves himself. For no one ever hated his own flesh, but nourishes and cherishes it, just as the Lord *does* the church." (Eph. 5:28-29)

The duty to preserve the life of others.
"For so it was, while Jezebel massacred the prophets of the LORD, that Obadiah had taken one hundred prophets and hidden them, fifty to a cave, and had fed them with bread and water."
1 Kings 18:4

The duty to resist all thoughts and purposes and subdue all passions which tend to the unjust taking away of anyone's life.
(That's the scholarly way to say "don't let my actions or thoughts lead to sin.")
We spent time on day one and three concerning this duty. Jesus addressed the

anger at the heart of murder, and we also talked about the duty of forgiveness regardless of another's actions.

"Be angry, and do not sin": do not let the sun go down on your wrath, nor give place to the devil." Eph. 4:26-27

The duty to comfort the distressed and protect and defend the innocent.
"Now we exhort you, brethren, warn those who are unruly, comfort the fainthearted, uphold the weak, be patient with all." 1 Thess. 5:14

"for I was hungry and you gave Me food; I was thirsty and you gave Me drink; I was a stranger and you took Me in;" Matthew 25:35

Not only are we commanded not to murder, from these passages we see the duties Scripture requires of us in response to the sixth command. Allow God to challenge you today!

The Measure of our Forgiveness

Daily Scripture Passage: Genesis 3:1-5
"Now the serpent was more cunning than any beast of the field which the LORD God had made. And he said to the woman, "Has God indeed said, 'You shall not eat of every tree of the garden'?"
And the woman said to the serpent, "We may eat the fruit of the trees of the garden; but of the fruit of the tree which is in the midst of the garden, God has said, 'You shall not eat it, nor shall you touch it, lest you die.'"
Then the serpent said to the woman, "You will not surely die. For God knows that in the day you eat of it your eyes will be opened, and you will be like God, knowing good and evil." NKJV

Thought to Consider: The Serpent's Whisper

This week we have discussed not only the issue of murder, but also the issue of hatred and anger. Take up the paper on any given day and you will see clearly the wrong expression of anger as individuals harm one another both physically and emotionally. Often these individual cite that they had no other option and were only acting out the only alternative left. The taking of a life is warranted in their minds, because they viewed it as the only option.

Today, we join together again in studying the call to honor life and forgive others. We are going to touch on an issue often driven by emotion when there seems to be no other options. This issue relates to the value of life and how abortion disregards that right. We have discussed anger and how we are to treat others, but today I want to discuss the controversial issue of abortion as it clearly relates to the sixth command. Today's devotional is an article from James Dobson's website by Carrie Gordon Earll. She works with Focus on the Family on issues relating to abortion.

The inestimable value of human life is a basic tenet of the Christian Worldview. Once you recognize that all human life exists to represent the image of God on earth (Genesis 1:27), the tragedy of abortion takes on new proportions. However, for many women who experience an undesired pregnancy, the concept of human life as sacred rings hollow, offering little tangible support for those considering choices in an abortion-friendly culture. The value of that tiny life growing in a woman's womb loses distinction amidst her own needs and circumstances. God's universal message declaring His likeness in humanity is crowded out by other voices around her: family, boyfriend, job or school. If you listen closely to these voices, you may recognize an ageless and familiar utterance articulated in the quietness of a whisper.

A biblical account of this whispering voice is found in Genesis when another woman's ear was tickled by a message contrary to God's. Her name was Eve, and her encounter with a wily serpent and subsequent choice to disregard God's instruction altered the course of human history.

The opening verse in Genesis chapter 3 recounts the story: "Now the serpent was more crafty than any of the wild animals the Lord God had made. He said to the woman, 'Did God really say, "You must not eat from any tree in the garden"?' You can almost hear the serpent whispering in an enticing tone: "Did God really say...?" The whisper challenged what Eve knew to be true, as is often the case with pregnant women considering abortion. As women, we know intuitively that it's not natural for us to kill our children. The very act of abortion disconnects us from our instinct to protect — not destroy — our young. If we listen to our intuition and the truth that is written on our hearts, we know that abortion is not our first choice. Circumstances may appear to make it our only choice; however, to do so violates who we are as women and mothers. Abortion is contrary to what we know to be true.

Like Eve before us, we consider the serpent's whisper and the unthinkable acceptance of abortion that it promotes. The serpent offered Eve half-truths that paved the way to justify disobeying God. Once she realized the heartbreak that resulted from her choice, Eve confessed what she failed to see at the time of her decision: "The serpent deceived me, and I ate."

The bitter fruit of abortion leaves more than an unpleasant aftertaste with those who eat it. Complications with future pregnancies, substance abuse and deep emotional regret represent only a few of the unintended consequences awaiting us when we are deceived by the serpent's whisper. Women whose ears are open to this murmuring soft voice need tangible support to counter its appeal — support that is available through a network of pro-life pregnancy resource centers across the nation. The voice of truth will always silence the lies, if only we will listen.

(Source: www.family.org by Carrie Gordon Earll)

The Measure of our Forgiveness

Daily Scripture Passage: Genesis 6:5-8, 9:1-6
5 *Then the LORD saw that the wickedness of man was great in the earth,*
and that every intent of the thoughts of his heart was only evil continually.
6 *And the LORD was sorry that He had made man on the earth, and He*
was grieved in His heart. 7 *So the LORD said, "I will destroy man whom I*
have created from the face of the earth, both man and beast, creeping
thing and birds of the air, for I am sorry that I have made them." 8 *But*
Noah found grace in the eyes of the LORD.

1 *So God blessed Noah and his sons, and said to them: "Be fruitful and*
multiply, and fill the earth. 2 *And the fear of you and the dread of you*
shall be on every beast of the earth, on every bird of the air, on all that
move on the earth, and on all the fish of the sea. They are given into your
hand. 3 *Every moving thing that lives shall be food for you. I have given*
you all things, even as the green herbs. 4 *But you shall not eat flesh with*
its life, that is, its blood. 5 *Surely for your lifeblood I will demand a*
reckoning; from the hand of every beast I will require it, and from the
hand of man. From the hand of every man's brother I will require the life
of man.

6 " *Whoever sheds man's blood,*
By man his blood shall be shed;
For in the image of God
He made man.

Thought to Consider: The Value of Human Life

"His heart was filled with pain." What incredible words those are in Genesis 6. God created mankind and because of the great wickedness of His creation, God's heart was filled with pain. In His judgment, He wiped mankind from the face of the earth. Yet in His mercy, He rescued one family because of the righteousness of Noah. As we come out on the other side of the flood we read the instructions that God gives to Noah. The first is this: be fruitful and increase in number and fill the earth. I am always amazed at the big families that were so common years ago, but this is quite a task God has given Noah and his family. They are to fill the earth! Following that command, God instructs Noah concerning their diet. Then comes the instruction that I want to focus on in this section. He says, “Whoever sheds the blood of man, by man shall his blood be shed; for in the image of God has God made man.”

As D. James Kennedy says in his book “Why the Ten Commandments Matter, “Through these words, God reveals His deep concern about the sanctity of the life he created. Human life is so important to Him that He issued a universal law. It was not given solely to the chosen Jews or any other group. It was given to the entire new world and has never been countermanded.”

God values human life because we were created in His image. No longer was the human race to act in the wickedness seen prior to the flood. Instead, life was to be valued above all else. God does not issue this command simply because He was looking for another rule for the checklist. He issues this command because of His great love for His creation. God values human life. We see this demonstrated in Matthew 6:26 where Jesus says, “Look at the birds of the air, for they neither sow nor reap nor gather into barns; yet your heavenly Father feeds them. Are you not of more value than they?” To murder is, as D. James Kennedy says, “a grievous sin because it is an attack upon those who are made in His image.”

My own appreciation of this command was so heightened when I understood the “Measure of Love” found in this command. This is not simply a law against a sinful act of man, it is a revelation of the love of God for mankind. When we understand the depth of this love, it propels us outward in loving others as we desire to be loved. Rather act in hatred and anger, we act in love and forgiveness. Rather than carry out vengeance and revenge, we choose forgiveness and restoration. Are those easy choices? By no means. To respond in love calls on our deep faith in God’s ability to teach us how to live in the liberty that we are offered in Christ. Forgiveness isn’t natural, it’s supernatural. It’s God doing through us what only He can do.

God values life and commands that we do the same. How will that principle affect how you treat someone today?

Connecting with the Commandments
WEEK SIX

Parents: *As you walk through today's commandment with your children, take time to read through this material and adapt this to your child's age. This will not be a verbatim lesson. Rather, I have presented some guidance on how you might approach this very common issue in raising children – dealing with anger!*

Opening Activity: As we begin today, tell me some of the things that occur at school that really make you mad. What are some things that really bother you? How have you have reacted to those things that have made you mad or those things that have bothered you? How did that situation end? The truth is, all of us have experienced times when we were upset or angry. So, today we are going to talk about what the Bible says about our anger and how we are to react when we are upset.

Purpose of Activity: This week the adults have been studying about God's command not to murder, but what we have also studied is the fact that this is a command against hatred or anger towards others. When God says that we are not to murder, that also means that He does not want us to hate or act out our anger against others.

Dealing with our Anger
Because we all get angry at some point, the real issue becomes how we respond to that anger. So today, we're going to talk about ways that we can do positive things that will help us respond in a good way to anger.

Stopping Anger – In 2011, a movie called "Unstoppable" came out on DVD and it is based on a real-life story of a CSX train worker getting off the train in 2001 after he thought he had put on the brake. Instead, he had turned the throttle up. So instead of stopping the train, the train went full speed ahead without anybody in it. The movie is about how someone got back on board and stopped the train before it hurt anyone.
In the same way that the train was running away in that movie, so our anger can be if we don't stop it. We can hurt someone just like that train was going to hurt folks if it wasn't stopped.

As hard as this can be at times, stopping our anger begins by sharing our emotions with others. Often, we need to share those emotions before we ever get to the point of reacting because sharing our thoughts in the midst of an emotional scene can be tough. So before you get into a tough spot with your anger, know that you can talk to us about what you are dealing with and we will do everything that we can to help you!

Time Out – In a sports competition, referees take a timeout sometimes in order to get things right. Also, coaches can request a timeout as well in order to sit down with the players and discuss a better way to approach the game. Sometimes we need to do that as well in order to better react in a situation. When our first emotion is anger, we need to stop and take a timeout. Otherwise, our reaction will likely be bad.
Think for a minute how you might "take a timeout" when you're in a tough situation. It might be that you count to 10 (or 100) to calm down. You might involve an adult so that they can help you. Either way, a time out can help you react better when you're mad.

Plumbing Issues: Having water in the house is a wonderful thing, as long as it is coming out at the right places. Not having to go outside to a well in order to get water is a great convenience. We only have to turn on the faucet and water is right there for us. But when things go wrong, water can come out everywhere. When that's happening, you want to quickly get to the source, which is the water shutoff valve for the whole house. Rather than try to fix the problem with water going everywhere, you want to get the water stopped! At times, when we are angry, we need to get to the source of the problem. Sometimes it's not that our siblings are making us mad, it's that we're tired and we need to rest. Other times, it's not that we're mad at our parents; we just had a really bad day at school and need a break. That's what it means to get to the source of our anger. At times we just need to talk about what's causing us to be angry. When we do that, we can help each other to understand what's going on in our lives and what's causing us to react as we are.

Choosing a Route: Before the days of GPS devices, we had to look at a map and decide on how we would get where we were going long before we ever even got in the car. We had to choose our route before we got going!
In dealing with our anger, a wise choice would be to figure out what route you are going to take to keep bad reactions from happening again. Just like picking out the roads you'll take on your next trip, so we need to pick out better options that will keep us from reacting negatively. That might mean you lose privileges, but sometimes we need to lose things that we like in order to get our attention on how we'll make wise choices in the future.

As a family, let's consider how we might love one another more rather than be filled with anger. We all do things wrong sometimes and we cause each other to get angry, but let's pray that God will give us a new desire to make things right with each other and get rid of our anger.

Pray to Close.

(End of "Connecting with the Commandments" time for this week)

Closing Thoughts on Dealing with Anger

Note to Readers: If anger is an issue that continues to plague your life, I encourage you to begin the process of healing from that anger. The first step is acknowledging the source of your anger. The root of your anger may be your hesitance to forgive someone that has wronged you. Realize today that your unwillingness to forgive imprisons you more than it does the one that offended you. Often we feel as though we are returning harm by refusing forgiveness, but the one that is most harmed is ourselves. We live in the captivity of that event that still leads to our anger today. Get to the root of your anger and be set free today.

I encourage you to read more on this issue by getting Gary Chapman's book, "Anger: Handling a Powerful Emotion in a Healthy Way". His book offers a Christian response to an issue that affects so many lives. Know that as I wrote these pages, I prayed for those that would be hearing these words. I prayed that God would set you free from your anger so that you could once again live in the freedom and joy of the Lord!

❧

THE MEASURE OF LOVE

CHAPTER SEVEN

The Measure of our Faithfulness

❧

The Measure of our Faithfulness

Introduction

The Ten Commandments have great application for our lives today. I pray that this is what you have discovered through our study of God's Ten Commandments. As we come to this seventh commandment I believe its application for our lives is all the more relevant in our day and time. In a world that treats marriage in much the same way as buying a new car – "try it and see if you like it" mentality - we need to be reminded of God's standard for our marriage relationships. We need to again revere the wonderful institution of marriage.

As we study this commandment in this chapter, I want to help you see how this commandment applies to each and every one of us, regardless of our marital status. If you are married, you have the duty of protecting your marriage and the marriage of others. If you are single, it is your duty to hold in high regard the marriage of others and to never endanger that union.

Principles of Scripture are rarely exclusive to one passage or section of Scripture and that is certainly true in relation to the commandment against adultery. God's instructions regarding marriage are found throughout Scripture. In one passage, Ephesians 5:3, we read that we should not have a hint of sexual immorality. There is no doubt that this verse applies to everyone. So I urge you to realize that the 7th commandment applies to every one of us, regardless of your marital situation.

Two Separate Studies - Men & Women's Study

As we approached this chapter of study I had the desire to discuss the issues of this command as they individually relate to men and women. In order to do that, our format will be different in this chapter. As you will notice, day one is a Men's Study. The following days of that section are specifically geared toward men and how this commandment applies to their lives. Men and women, you are welcome to read any of this material, but understand that one is designed for you and one for the other. The Women's Study begins following day five of the Men's Study. There you will find 5 days of material written by my wife, Amanda Hodge, specifically geared toward women. I pray God challenges you during your study of this commandment.

ക്ക

The Measure of our Faithfulness

Men's Study

Introduction

In this chapter, you are going to have the opportunity to begin to take bold steps forward in your faith and in your relationship with your spouse or future spouse. My purpose in this chapter is going to be the application of this commandment through intentional steps on your behalf one day at a time. Men, this is not the chapter for surface discussions and religious facades. We are going to discuss what we need to be doing as men to protect the fidelity of our marriages. For those of you who are single, this is an opportunity to begin to place hedges around your life that will forever change your future relationships, regardless of whether your marry.

In this chapter, we will talk about the topics of sexual purity and integrity in marriage. Your immediate response may be that you don't need this material, that your marriage is fine as it is. Let me congratulate you on your wonderful relationship while at the same time encourage you to realize that your relationship can only grow. Imagine if all of the focus of your attention and affection, which we will talk about in this chapter, were suddenly focused on your wife alone. Imagine the difference that it would make in your marriage relationship in the way you communicate with one another and enjoy one another's presence.

I only ask that you open your heart to what God wants to teach you this in this chapter. Anything of value is costly, and it might mean that this week you need to trade in pride and resistance for honesty and growth.

Pray that God will challenge you and look forward to the resulting change within your marriage and/or other relationships!

The Measure of our Faithfulness - Men's Study

Daily Scripture Passage: Exodus 20:14
14 "You shall not commit adultery.

Ephesians 5:3
But among you there must not be even a hint of sexual immorality, or of any kind of impurity, or of greed, because these are improper for God's holy people.

Thought to Consider: Getting to the Heart of the Issue

Today is the beginning devotional for the men's study. Ladies, while you are welcome to read this material, I encourage you to skip over to the introduction to the women's study and begin there as we all seek to be challenged by God's standards for our relationships.

To approach the issue central to the seventh commandment with timidity and fear of offending would be an injustice to the urgency of God's command. With that in mind, let's get to the heart of the issue. The issue is not unhappiness in marriage. The issue is not incompatibility of mates or irreconcilable differences, as is so often the cited reason for Hollywood divorces. I heard a speaker say recently that you did not take a glance at your wife and say when you first met, "Now she would be perfect for making me miserable for the rest of my life." Instead you said to everyone that knew you, "You don't know her like I do!" Along the same lines, I do not believe that spouses wrote in their vows, "I take you as my starter wife until someone else comes along that is a better fit for me." There was surely fascination, love, and intimacy at one point in your marriage. Your vows were words of an open, mutual commitment rather than fine print, I believe that the source of adultery is not the issues of incompatibility and such. I believe the irreducible minimum is lust and coveting. That's the heart of the issue. I'm sorry men, but you have all been plagued with it, some more than others. Lust is defined as, "intense longing or personal desire" (Merriam Webster Dictionary). If we follow that definition, within God's framework of marriage, it fuels passion within your relationship and is the excitement that we all looked forward to for years! But outside of marriage it is as Joshua Harris (from his book *Not Even a Hint*) defines, "craving sexually what God has forbidden". And so as I speak of lust from this point forward, I am not referring to the God ordained passion of a man for his wife. Instead, what I am referring to is how Joshua Harris defines it - outside of the context of marriage. But according to Webster's definition we also see how coveting can play a role in the measure of our faithfulness. In the same way that coveting can lead you into financial ruin, so it can lead your marriage to destruction. Let's get to the heart of the issue in this chapter.

Read Ephesians 5:3

"Not even a hint" That's a high standard! You might begin at this point making a game plan. After all, that's what guys do. We address the problem and create a plan. But before you find yourself frustrated by the repeated failure of your plan, keep in mind that any plan attempted in your own strength will be fatally affected by your sin nature. If you determined today that you would no longer look upon any woman with lust, surely your determination would be replaced with discouragement rather quickly. You see, this is not an instruction God has given in the Ten Commandments, and also through Paul, that we are to commit to accomplish as a work of our flesh. It is only possible through the power of God at work within us. That is true with all of the commandments. My obedience is the measure of my love for Him, but my obedience demonstrates even more so my *relationship* to Him, because otherwise I would be incapable of that very obedience. Now that may sound complicated, but it is summed up like this - You love Him so you follow Him. He loves you so He gives you the *strength* to follow Him.

But why is the recognition of that fact important? Because it helps you to live in freedom. If you believe that you will tame your wandering eyes, that you will fence in your wandering mind, that you will conquer lust in your own strength, you will surely fail. But if you commit this area of your life today to Him, He promises to walk with you as you make those commitments.

In the years before the original writing of this material I had primarily worked only with teenage guys on the subject of sexual purity. In fact, we used Joshua Harris' book to deal with this as the topic of a retreat. In the process I made an interesting observation. I observed that the adult leaders were just as challenged by the topic as the students. So this is not an issue solely to be dealt with around teenagers. It is an issue that continually plagues men seeking to live for the Lord.

In that crowd of teenagers many years ago, more than once the comment surfaced, "It's just too hard to get away from this temptation." What they were referring to was the constant bombardment by media in print, television, and web with sexually explicit images. It is in the context of this desensitized society that God says, "Thou shall not commit adultery." The standard remains. So as we consider the application of the commandment in this chapter, we need to be honest enough to say, "God, I need your help in my marriage" or "God, I need your help as a single man!"

Men, when the pipe bursts, the engine quits, or the computer crashes, it is time to skip all the conversation and just get to the task. That's what we're doing today, men. Let's weed through all of the pride and piety and just be transparent before the Lord. He already knows our hearts. How could we honor Him more than by recognizing where we may be weak and allowing Him to change us? Join me on the journey - Not Even a Hint!!

What is your initial response to the subject of today's devotional? Do you see where it might apply in your life?

Where is there a "hint" of sexual immorality within your life? You might not want to write that down, but take a moment to consider that question. Is it in your television viewing? Is it in your time on the internet? Ask God to reveal where you are allowing a "hint" of immorality.

Do you think there is room for growth within your marriage? In what ways?

The Measure of our Faithfulness - Men's Study

Daily Scripture Passage: Romans 13:14
Rather, clothe yourselves with the Lord Jesus Christ, and do not think about how to gratify the desires of the sinful nature.

Thought to Consider: Faithful and Faithfully Tempted, Pt.1

"But put on the Lord Jesus Christ, and make no provision for the flesh, to *fulfill its* lusts." (Rom. 13:14, NKJV, emphasis mine)

As we begin our study today, I want to encourage you, men, to consider investing in your marriage through intentional marriage building opportunities. These might be found in events like "Weekend to Remember" by Dennis and Barbara Rainey. There are even Christian cruises (Love Like You Mean It Cruise) geared specifically towards building marriages. Though events like these may change in the years following the revision of this book, the basic idea remains the same – invest in your marriage. Plan a time when you can just be with your spouse this week in a time of positive interaction. For those of you who are reading this material and are not married, I encourage those of you who are anticipating marriage to take note of this advice as a great tool for your relationship toolbox.

For the next two days we are going to expand on our commitment to be faithful to our wives. Unfortunately, with our desire to be faithful is also the guarantee that we will be faithfully tempted. Temptation will not give up the fight and leave us alone. As we consider this, I love the way Romans 13:14 is translated in the New King James Version. The key words "make no provision" are crucial to our application of this passage to our lives. Making no provision means that we might need to remove the source of temptation from our homes, and remove it from in front of our eyes, if possible. If I am going to adultery-proof my marriage, then I have to make no provision for the sin nature that would draw me away from my wife.

Again, based on Joshua Harris' book, *Not Even a Hint*, we are going to talk about areas where you might make provision for lust and how you need to put the guard up!

1. Tempting locations
   It might be a bookstore where you see inappropriate material. It might be the video rental place or channels on your cable/satellite subscription where you pass by inappropriate material. It might be vacationing at the beach where your covenant with your eyes will be tempted. Do you have to get rid of all these places? No. But you need to begin today to be aware of the temptation in all these places and "make no provision" for the flesh. You may choose to change one or more of these. Do what the Lord convicts you to do.

2. Television
   Does your remote tend to stop as you pass by a channel with an inappropriate image on it? I would venture to say it has and you probably felt guilty about it, but you find yourself venturing back to that channel once again. "Make no provision" through your television habits. You may need to block channels or even change your cable/satellite subscription. Do what it takes to be above reproach in what you allow your eyes to watch.

3. Internet
   This is not third on Joshua Harris' list, but I think this one is right up there with locations and television. Unfortunately for all of us, the internet has brought crude, despicable images right into our homes via the internet. Unsuspecting emails can expose your eyes to things you never imagined. In this area, make sure you "make no provision" for the stumbling block of the internet. Keep your computer out in the family room where anyone can walk over and see what you're looking at. Limit your "bored" time on the internet. There are even filters available such as "bsafehome.com" that can help with filtering. Make it a priority.

4. Print Media
   The bombardment of perverse print media may not be all that apparent without your being sensitive to it. How often do you pass through the grocery aisle and are confronted with inappropriate images? How often have you received a perfectly legitimate sales catalog only to be exposed to scantily clad women? Watch your eyes when you check mail or read a magazine. Make no provision!

Why are all those things important?
Each of these are important because they are all steps Satan will use in desensitizing you to sin. While you may not find it harmful to watch an

"inappropriate" program or movie, it is only a progression. Satan uses these everyday points of temptation to desensitize you to sin. Not many men would ever say they envisioned themselves eating with a female co-worker or friend and allowing that relationship to venture into unfaithfulness. However, what was likely true was that they made provision for their flesh and turned away from God's commands.

The Bible says, "Then, when desire has conceived, it gives birth to sin; and sin, when it is full-grown, brings forth death" (James 1:15). Don't let the desire give birth to greater sin! Commit today to a plan for the battle. Whether lust is an issue for you today or not, don't allow Satan an inch in who you are as a man - or he will become your ruler!

❧

The Measure of our Faithfulness - Men's Study

Daily Scripture Passage: Exodus 20:14
Job 31:1
"I have made a covenant with my eyes;
Why then should I look upon a young woman?

Thought to Consider: Faithful and Faithfully Tempted, Pt.2

Job truly was an incredible man. He was described as "blameless and upright; he feared God and shunned evil." While we all would appreciate that description by God Himself, none of us would want to endure the trials that Job faced to demonstrate his faithfulness. Nonetheless, we can use the life of Job as an example of a godly man to be followed.

In his book *Every Man's Battle*, Fred Stoeker writes, "Job was just a man! As you realize that, these precious words should gloriously fill your soul: *If he can do it, so can I*. God wants you to know that in your manhood as He created it, you, too, can rise above sexual temptation."

Men, you may be very confident in your marriage relationship. If that is the case, congratulations. But is it possible that your selection of movies, television shows, or print materials is inching closer and closer to the line of lust? That's what Job refused to be a part of. I imagine if a movie showed an

inappropriate and unsuspected scene, that he would have turned his eyes in order to keep the covenant he had made with God, or even stood up and walked out of the movie!

I taught this principle to the students in our church a number of years ago, as well as the principle of "bouncing your eyes". What that means is that when you see a young lady in person, media, or print, that you quickly bounce your eyes onto something else. Try checking out at the grocery store and you'll apply this principle really quickly. One of the students made the comment, "I'm going to look like a ping pong ball walking down the hall at school." That might be the case, but I'd rather look silly than sinful!

Job was successful in his endeavor to covenant with his eyes. Do you know how I know? Because no man who failed in this endeavor would make the statement in Job 31:9-11 that Job did. Job was clearly disgusted with his sin. He determined to change his ways and the result is that his marriage was stronger than ever.

He declared, "If my heart has been enticed by a woman, or if I have lurked at my neighbor's door, then may my wife grind another man's grain, and may other men sleep with her. For that would have been shameful, a sin to be judged."

Men, we need to seriously evaluate our commitment to purity. We need to be men that are resolute in our determination to honor God's commandments for the sake of our marriages and our families.

There is wonderful news today as you apply this passage. As we make a covenant with our eyes, we will begin to turn our full attention onto our spouses. Picture two buckets in which you pour water. Each time you lovingly desire your wife, you fill that bucket with a few drops of water. On the contrary, when you lust, in whatever means, you fill the other bucket with a few drops of water. Now imagine the result of a covenant of your eyes is going to make. Rather than spreading those drops of water over two buckets, it will now flow into one bucket. You can expect your wife to notice a difference! Whereas you once only poured a few drops of water in the bucket illustrating your marriage, now you'll be focusing all your attention on her!

If you are committing to this today, then you may want to warn your spouse that your love for her will be stronger, your desire for her will be greater, and your relationship will be unlike it has ever been before. Why? Because you have made a covenant with your eyes to turn all of your attention on that ONE person that God planned for you.

Single men, the task before you is difficult. As you seek the one that God would have for you, or as you live content single, you are equally accountable to this principle to which Job committed. Today, will you make that commitment? It will forever change your future relationships.

ಹಿ

The Measure of our Faithfulness - Men's Study

Daily Scripture Passage: 1 Thessalonians 5:22
"Avoid every kind of evil."

Thought to Consider: Planting Hedges in our Daily Lives

Today I want to highlight a resource that I discovered several years ago entitled "Loving Your Marriage Enough to Protect It" (Now reprinted under the title of "Hedges"). It was written by Jerry B. Jenkins, co-author of the Left Behind books. In the book, Jenkins talks about steps that he intentionally takes to protect his marriage. He calls these steps "hedges".

- Whenever he needs to meet or dine or travel with an unrelated woman, he adds a third person. Based on 1 Thessalonians 5:22, Jenkins wants to avoid the appearance of evil. In turn, he avoids the evil itself. I believe this is a great practice that we would do well to observe within our own lives. Think not only of the act of sin, but the less noticeable steps toward that sin and avoid them!
- Be careful about touching. Only embrace dear friends or relatives, and only in front of others. While our church family does not need to become a rigid, loveless group, hugs between church family ought to be appropriate. But if touching is for personal pleasure and not for mutual friendship, the line should be drawn. That's what Jenkins addresses in this "hedge".
- Some compliments don't pay. If she looks nice in that clothing, then compliment the clothing, not her. That is inappropriate.

- Avoid flirtation or suggestive comments, even in jest. This is the testing ground for adultery. Never should God's children be a part of comments that open the door for the devil's traps. As Jenkins says, "Everyone knows that funny people speak the truth through humor." I believe humor is often used as the vehicle for inappropriate comments. Avoid those comments.
- Remember your vows to your wife. For those that are single, respect the vows made by someone's wife. Remembering your vows might be through writing those vows again to your wife in a nice card or through simply saying encouraging words to your wife based on the commitment made in your vows. Whatever way this plays out, remind yourself and your spouse often of the commitment you have made to one another.
- Quality Time vs. Quantity Time. Jenkins makes a great point in this chapter about our simply being present in the home physically but in no other way. We arrive home exhausted from work, stressed and maxed out, and simply wanting to stop for the day. We are present for quantity time, but hardly quality time. Think this week how your time with your wife can be quality time - time that is focused on her and what is going on in her world.

Believe me, I have only scratched the surface of the what Jenkins deals with in his book on the subject. The reason I have pulled so much from his book today is, first of all, to peak your interest in the book. Secondly, to give you a jumpstart on considering the hedges that exist in your own life. How high are the hedges within your own life? If the opportunity presented itself to compromise your standards, how well would the hedges within your own life protect you from that attack? You may be walking blindly right now under the assumption that the seventh command will never affect you, and I pray that it will not. But the best way to ensure that you are not a victim of adultery is to begin planting hedges today that will protect you. Yours will be different than Jerry Jenkins' or Michael Hodge's. But the purpose will be the same - to protect the marriage that God has given!

The Measure of our Faithfulness - Men's Study

Daily Scripture Passage: Matthew 5:27-28
"You have heard that it was said, 'Do not commit adultery.' But I tell you that anyone who looks at a woman lustfully has already committed adultery with her in his heart."

Thought to Consider: Actions and Consequences

In 1985, Michael J. Fox starred in the runaway hit "Back to the Future". In the movie, Fox plays Marty McFly who travels back in time. His accidental destination was 1955 where his parents first met and were later married. Marty quickly realizes that his actions could permanently change history, primarily his own. If he is not able to convince his future mother and father to fall in love in 1955, Marty's own existence is in danger. There was little doubt that his every action had serious consequences.

Consequence can be a great motivator, and a fitting one when we are discussing the seventh commandment. I read about a counselor who asked the question, "What effect will my actions have if I go through the door called Desire?" Ron Mehl records the counselors response to that question in Mehl's book, "The Tender Commandments". The counselor came up with 14 resulting actions:

- I will grieve the One who redeemed me.
- I will drag His sacred name through the mud.
- I will have to look Jesus in the eye one day and give an account of my actions.
- I will inflict untold hurt on my wife, who is my best friend and who has been faithful to me.
- I will lose my wife's respect, love, and trust.
- I will hurt my beloved daughters.
- I will destroy my example and my credibility
- I will lose my wife and children forever.
- I will shame my family.
- I will lose my own self-respect.

- I could form memories and flashbacks that plague future intimacy with my spouse.
- I could reap consequences of diseases.
- I could cause a pregnancy that would be a lifelong reminder of my sin.
- I could invoke lifelong shame and embarrassment on myself.

In our passage for today we see Jesus raising the bar on the seventh commandment. God is not interested in heartless obedience that moves as close to the line of law breaking as possible without “stepping over”. What Jesus helped us to see was that God desires our total obedience in regard to the seventh command - not just in our final actions - but in the motives of the heart that lead to sin. Jesus went to the heart of the issue - lust. That’s what we talked about on day one.

I can remember a time when I was young when I ventured off on my bicycle for a trip through the neighborhood. That was my normal routine during the summer months. As long as I checked in from time to time, it was perfectly alright. But on that particular day I lost track of time. I was at the “trouble” kid’s house. He was an older kid who was known for getting into trouble quite a bit. But I thought he was neat because he knew how to do tricks on his bike that I couldn’t do and just because he was older. What I did not realize was happening during my visit with my neighborhood friend was an all-out search for me. My mother had called all of her friends and they were scouring the neighborhood looking for me. Late in the day I saw my mother pull up in my friend’s driveway. This was not good. Mom didn’t usually come looking for me. I knew it was not going to be good. But the punishment was interesting. My mom made me write sentences saying, “I will not run away from home” over and over. It is very clear that she had run out of the creativity and energy to teach and punish three boys, but this was unlike any punishment I’d ever had. I mean writing, come on mom?! So there I was, sitting at the kitchen table, writing “I will not run away from home” over and over. But do you know that I thought twice about staying gone all day next time! I had better plans for my evenings than writing that crazy sentence over and over. I realized that my actions would result in consequences and I did not like those crazy consequences.

When it comes to the seventh command, we are being instructed to avoid adultery because of the consequences. Maybe today you need to realize, like Marty McFly and our counselor in today’s devotional, that actions have consequences, and that the consequences are not worth the action.

I do not know what you are going through in your marriage right now. Your days and evenings at home may be miserable right now. Argument and strife are the only conversations that ever take place. Can I challenge you today to carefully choose your steps. Don't take a step in your anger or rebellion that will reap consequences beyond what you can imagine. Your actions today can affect tomorrow. Why not begin today looking for the light at the end of the tunnel and begin taking steps toward healing that will forever affect tomorrow. You may be the spouse that has to initiate it. Prayerfully take a step toward your marriage today! That action will have great consequences!!

As a follow-up to this chapter's material, I want to invite you to be incredibly honest with yourself, and with your wife if you choose to do so. Take the following quiz. If you are offended by this quiz, then you have missed the point of this chapter! The world is not ashamed of what it is throwing at us. We need to be spiritually mature enough to fight the devil's attacks!

If you have been honest on this quiz today, I want to invite you to use this as part of your game plan for protecting your marriage. Recognize your weaknesses and start building hedges around those weaknesses.

Level of Vulnerability			
Source of Temptation	High	Medium	Low
A Woman's Appearance			
A Woman's Dress			
Pornography			
Magazines			
Books			
Cable Television			
Movies			
Health Clubs			
Flirting			
Friendly Conversation			
Swimming Events			
Art			
Posters			
Other:_______________			

(Quiz is based on "Loving Your Marriage Enough to Protect It" by Jerry Jenkins.)

ര

The Measure of our Faithfulness

Women's Study

by Amanda Hodge

Introduction

I am extremely fortunate to have a Godly wife who seeks to honor our relationship and guard our marriage through intentional acts of love. She is going to tell you that we have not figured it all out, and she is right. Our relationship is not perfect, but I wouldn't trade it for anything. She lovingly supports my ministry and my role as father to our children. I believe my life theme verse is Philippians 3:12 where Paul says, "not that I have already obtained all this…" Amanda and I had not obtained all that we wrote in these devotionals in 2006, but they *are* principles that we continue to strive towards in 2011and beyond just the same.

Ladies, enjoy these devotionals in this chapter, written especially for you by my wife, Amanda. Much of what she is going to be talking about comes from a great book that she read during the summer of 2006 entitled "Becoming the Woman of His Dreams". Now there's a book that you want your wife to check out of the library!! I pray that the words of reflection upon this book that Amanda shares will be a challenge to your faith and your relationship with your spouse. God Bless!

Just as with the Men's Study, this material is written with both the married and single women in mind. Though the material will lean heavier in the direction of those that are married, the attempt has been made to find application in both situations. So we hope that this material speaks to both audiences as you read this week.

The Measure of our Faithfulness - Women's Study

Daily Scripture Passage: Genesis 2:18
"The LORD God said, "It is not good for the man to be alone. I will make a helper suitable for him."

Proverbs 31

Thought to Consider: Qualities Every Man Desires

"There should be such a oneness between you and your marriage that when one weeps, the other tastes salt." Fourteen years ago I saw these words matted and framed in a Christian book store. They impressed me so much that I had them printed on our wedding programs. After twelve years of marriage, I still take these words to heart. My husband, Michael, and I have a great marriage and a wonderful friendship but we don't have it all figured out! We have taken steps that have helped us improve. So when Michael asked me to write this devotional back in 2006 for the women, I was excited about the chance to perhaps learn more myself. But I must also admit that I felt a little nervous, unsure, frantic, and unqualified. Today as I reflect back on what I wrote several years ago, I am reminded once again that God is most interested in my availability, not my ability. So, with God's help, I pray these words will challenge you those of you who are married as well as those of you who are now single.

If you asked your husband or fiancé, "What would you consider as the woman of your dreams?" - how would he respond? You're thinking, "If he's got any brains at all he'd say, 'You of course!'" That's the question asked in the book from which much of this devotional material is taken. Thankfully, God has already laid this out for us in His Word. Proverbs 31 describes the excellent wife. This gal has it all! What a challenge! In her book, "Becoming the Woman of His Dreams", Sharon Jaynes attempts to give us qualities that men long to see in a wife. According to hundreds of interviews and surveys, these were the qualities that lead husbands to praise their wife at the beginning and end of their lives and all the days in between. Over the next few days, let's study those qualities and ask God to teach us how they might improve our marriages, or honor other's marriages, and keep us far from adultery.

Quality No. 1 - Prayer.

Donald Kauffman says, "A good marriage is not a contract between two persons but a sacred covenant between three." We cannot be the Proverbs 31 woman without prayer. We can do nothing without the power of the Holy Spirit. When we see problems arising in our marriages or we struggling in the fact that we are now single, many times we try to fix them on our own. Then when all else fails, we finally get around to praying about it. Why is prayer many times our last resort when it is truly our only hope? Look at Genesis 2:18. God has created us to be helpers. Without Eve, Adam was lacking. Without Adam, Eve was lacking. Paul says this in 1 Corinthians 11:11. God created us to depend on and complement each other. Jayne points out that "Helper" (woman) is derived from the Hebrew word used of God and the Holy Spirit. When we consider that the same descriptive title is used for both God and woman, we can see "helper" as a position of honor. This is how God set it up - not man! Just as Christ is our intercessor, we too are intercessors for our husbands. As a prayer warrior or intercessor, we have great responsibility. No one else is more qualified to pray for our husbands than we are as wives. For those that are anticipating marriage, now is the time to begin praying for that one God has chosen for you. Pray daily that he would be the man of God whose leadership will place God at the center of your family.

We see in God's Word that a marriage between a man and a woman is the visual reminder of the union between Christ and the Church (Rev. 19:7). Who would like to destroy this living example (John 10:10)? Satan is our real enemy. Growing up, my mother would frequently quote Ephesians 6:12. When we struggle in our marriages it's so much easier to blame specific causes of the problems. We need to pray against Satan's evil attacks against this union. Pray that it will be a God centered union. As Sharon Jaynes says, "Praying for your husband is synonymous with praying for yourself. When we are married we are joined together as one flesh. Therefore, praying for your husband is like praying for the other half of your being."

As we consider this call to prayer for our spouses, there are those reading this study that have outlived spouses and now face new challenges in life. But rather than view this invitation from today's study as irrelevant to your life stage, why not use this as an invitation to pray for the marriages of loved ones facing some of the challenges that you walked through in your own marriage. Consider those within your church and pray for their marriages. I know my husband and I love to hear that people are praying for us!

There's nothing that annoys my husband more than a car that dings, clicks or rattles. Is this what you sound like to your husband - a nag? Look at Proverbs 19:13, 25:24. Prayer is the best way to prevent this from happening. Instead of nagging, become persistent in your prayers. Don't forget that God answers prayers in His time. Our husbands are His workmanship, not ours. We often want to create or shape our men into what we want, forgetting God's plan. In Stormie Omartian's book, "The Power of a Praying Wife," one of the biggest points she makes is that change must begin in our own hearts. Many times we pray for our husbands with the wrong motives (James 4:3). Jaynes suggests reading 1 Corinthians 13 as we begin to pray for ourselves in becoming the woman of our man's dreams.

1. How does Paul encourage us to pray in 1 Thessalonians 5:17-18?

2. Have you been faithful in praying for your husband? If you're not married are there friends or family members you can commit to praying for?

3. If you are willing to make a commitment to pray for your husband every day, fill in your names in the following:

I __________________ (your name), commit to pray for my husband __________________ (his name) every day. I commit to pray for his spiritual growth, for him to have divine wisdom, and for him to grow closer to Christ. I also commit to pray for myself, that I may be the wife my husband needs.

4. Pick one of the following passages of scripture and put your husband's name in the prayer: 2 Timothy 1:3, Colossians 1:3, Ephesians 6:18.

The Measure of our Faithfulness - Women's Study

Daily Scripture Passage: Ephesians 5:22-25 (NKJV)
"Wives, submit to your own husbands, as to the Lord. For the husband is head of the wife, as also Christ is head of the church; and He is the Savior of the body. Therefore, just as the church is subject to Christ, so let the wives be to their own husbands in everything.
Husbands, love your wives, just as Christ also loved the church and gave Himself for her"

Proverbs 31:22
She makes coverings for her bed;
she is clothed in fine linen and purple.

Thought to Consider: Respecting your Husband

On day one we discussed the first of seven qualities that Sharon Jaynes discusses as qualities men long to see in their wives. Today we will look at the second quality - respect and submission.

Quality No. 2 – Respect and Submission

R-E-S-P-E-C-T. Sing with me now! Why is that Aretha Franklin song so popular? Sure it has a good tune but respect is one thing every human longs for! Somewhere between picking up dirty socks and moving that pair of shoes for the third time, we tend to lose that sense of respect. I once read an interesting suggestion. Each time you do that stinky load of laundry, take that chance to thank God for the opportunity. Pray that God will guide your husband's footsteps throughout that day.

Look at Ephesians 5:33. God's Word says that we must respect our husbands just as they are to love us. "But," you say, "you don't know my husband. How can I respect him if he doesn't respect himself?" It may seem impossible but the same God that parted the Red Sea and caused the walls of Jericho to fall can give you the power you need. Just as I learned in a study of *Experiencing God*, we will experience God and His power *after* we take that first step of obeying Him!

Now to the issue no one likes to discuss - submission. Why is it such an issue when God has so much to say about it in His Word? We as women are capable of leadership, but in the marriage union, God's design is for us to have a different role. Do you truly believe God's word is true and inspired? Then what does Ephesians 5:22-23 say? We can't pick and choose what we want to obey from God's word. However, this does not mean the husband is the dictator and we are doormats. Continue reading through verse 25. Just as Christ has loved the church, the husbands should love us! Christ loved us enough to die for us. Our husbands should have the same sacrificial love.

What if your husband fails or messes up as the head of the household? Jaynes says, "We have the opportunity to serve up love on a silver platter." If I see my husband has made a mistake, I try and do one of two things: (1) Stay silent. Never say, "I told you so," or "you should have just let me do it!" (2) Try and encourage him with kind words. He feels bad enough without me reminding him of his mistakes! Remember to *continue* to pray for him!

One of my favorite artists, Shaun Groves, sings a song that says, "I'd rather be a pauper than a prince - living without you." Another way we can show respect is by being content with our financial situations. If the wife is constantly complaining about what she doesn't have, the husband begins to think he isn't the man she'd always hoped for. In the perfect garden, who told Eve that there was more? Satan. Remember who our real enemy is!

We can respect our man in the way we take care of our appearance. I've not met a man yet that admits that he enjoys living with a bum of a wife! (Sure we all have those bad days.) A close friend told me years ago, "If you got a man, you gotta keep him!" For our first date, Michael and I left at 5:00 in the morning to take his friend to the airport in Atlanta. You'd better believe I was up at 4:00 in the morning getting all dolled up! I still try to take pride in the way I dress. As we all know, men were created to be visually stimulated. Do you dress to please your man? I always try to dress with my husband in mind. One fun thing that Michael and I used to do was to grab a clothing catalogue and I would mark all of the things that I liked and then have Michael do the same – just to see if we were on the same page. I know what you're thinking - it's cheap entertainment but it does help me to know his likes and dislikes in women's clothing. "An old barn always looks good with a little fresh paint," my dad always said. It doesn't take much effort or lots of money. Accent your best features. A little goes a long way. Don't forget to smile (and don't slump)! Look at Proverbs 31:22. The excellent wife is clothed in "fine linen and purple". She takes care of herself.

There are so many ways to respect your husband. Ask God to show you where you need help in this area.

1. Make a list of any ways that you have not been respecting your husband. What are you willing to change? Be specific.

2. Do you have a problem with submission in your marriage? Why or why not? How has our scripture reading for today helped you with this issue?

3. Choose one of the following verses and note what they say about the source of beauty: Psalm 9:8, Psalm 34:5, Proverbs 15:13, Isaiah 61:1-3.

4. Do you truly aim to please your husband in your appearance or are you aiming to please other people?

ಹಿಳು

The Measure of our Faithfulness - Women's Study

Daily Scripture Passage: 2 Corinthians 2:10-11
"If you forgive anyone, I also forgive him. And what I have forgiven—if there was anything to forgive—I have forgiven in the sight of Christ for your sake, in order that Satan might not outwit us. For we are not unaware of his schemes."

Thought to Consider: Admiring your Husband

Quality No. 3 - Admiration
In what ways do you adore or admire your husband? I can honestly say that I adore my husband for his desire to love and serve God with all his heart. Do you ever tell your husband that you appreciate him or tell him why he's so wonderful? Do you encourage him or do you degrade him when you're with friends? Where does he go for admiration and appreciation? Dr. Willard Harley says, "When a woman tells a man he's wonderful, that inspires him to achieve more. Admiration not only motivates, it also rewards the husband's existing achievements. A man expects and needs his wife to be his most enthusiastic fan. He draws confidence from her support and can usually achieve far more with her. Don't make your husband go outside your marriage for approval; he needs the perspective your appreciation gives him." Maybe this is hard for you to do because you're not used to it. Start small - maybe a "thank you". By all means be real! Truly mean what you say! Maybe you've gotten so used to criticizing and putting your husband down. You may have lots of "weeds to pull" before those hurts are gone!

One of those weeds might be forgiveness. Maybe there's a lot of forgiveness that needs to take place in your marriage - deep rooted bitterness! There are some things we certainly can't turn a blind eye to. Certain things must be addressed and dealt with perhaps through Christian counseling in order for this marriage to survive and thrive. C.S. Lewis says, "Everyone says forgiveness is a lovely idea until they have something to forgive." You can't have the marriage of your dreams without forgiveness. Look at 2 Corinthians 2:10-11. "Satan knows that as long as we hold a grudge, our earthly example of Christ and the Church (our marriage) will be marred and we will never experience the oneness God intended." My Dad used to sing a song taken from Psalm 139:23-24 that brought tears to my eyes and is still one of my favorites. "Search me, Oh God, and know my heart; test me and know my anxious thoughts. See if there is any offensive way in me and lead me in the way everlasting." Sometimes that pride is so hard to let go of! Maybe unforgiveness is deeply rooted and at home in your heart. Walls are built up in your marriage. Today, let this verse be a prayer from the depths of your heart.

I'm sure if you have children or grandchildren then you're not easily grossed out by much. One Sunday evening while at church, our son Jerrett (when he was 4 yrs. old) found a piece of gum in the trash can, dug it out, proceeded to pop it into his little mouth. Of course I was horrified but tried to remember that some germs are actually good for your children. Many times like our son, we tend to dig things out from the past in our marriages. Don't let your marriage become a full trash can! This is the advice Paul gives in Philippians 3:14. In Jaynes' book she says, "Forgiveness is a decision, not a feeling." You must forgive with prayer. "[Prayer] is a gentle tool of restoration appropriated through the prayers of a wife who longs to do right more than be right, and to give life more than to get even." After all, as Christ suffered through His last breath he prayed, "Father, forgive them, for they do not know what they are doing" (Luke 23:34). What a picture of love in a marriage!

Many times we are the ones who need to beg forgiveness. *Repent* is also an action, not a feeling. Tell your husband what you are going to do differently!

Allow God to work through you in your marriage. Allow him to break down those walls and shatter those barriers that keep you from a marriage that God intends for you to have.

How are we to forgive according to Ephesians 4:32 and Colossians 3:13? What does that look like to you? Is there something in your marriage that you can't seem to let go of? Write it down on a piece of paper, shred it or burn it and pray that God will help you release this to him.

ණ

The Measure of our Faithfulness - Women's Study

Daily Scripture Passage: Genesis 2:24
For this reason a man will leave his father and mother and be united to his wife, and they will become one flesh.

Thought to Consider: Serving and Communicating in Marriage

Quality No. 4 – Serving
How do you take care of your husband's needs? Do you count it a joy to do his laundry? I've shared with a friend before that I truly don't mind washing the clothes and I often don't mind the folding. But it's the putting away that I nearly despise! If I'm having a good day, I just may find it in my heart to put my husband's clothes away. How have you found ways in your marriage to serve your husband? We often hear it said that marriage takes 50/50 yet neither can agree on where the halfway mark is, so we sit and judge each other's performance. Who put the toilet seat down last? Who left the toothpaste in the sink? Who picked the shoes up out of the floor for the 30th time this week? Who took the garbage out last? Who changed the last diaper? Who cleaned the car out last? Why not try this contest: who can out-serve the other?

In washing the disciples' feet, Jesus set this example as He fulfilled the needs the others had failed to meet. He did what no one else was willing to do. Many times we are so worried that our husbands will get used to us being their "personal" maid that we don't even bother serving. When we serve our husbands, we are in effect serving Christ Himself. In her book, Jaynes says, "It may be entirely possible for you to serve your husband and not feel that you are receiving anything in return. However, your heavenly Father is always watching, and the measure you use to bless your husband will be used by your heavenly Husband to bless you in return."

Question: In what ways do you care for your husband's needs? Now go the extra mile. In what ways can you care for your husband's needs besides what you already do? Be creative.

Quality No. 5 – Communication
All men want to feel important, right? Then make him feel like it! Talk with him. Ask him questions that let him know you are truly interested in how his day went. Then, actively listen. Take an interest in what's going on in his life - his hobbies, his interests, his desires, his dreams. I've often heard it said , "If you can't beat 'em, join 'em." When we were in seminary, Michael became interested in model trains. So, we had a model train set on a big table that Michael had constructed. Sure, it only took up half of the dining area in our apartment. But, I sucked it up and helped him paint the model buildings and gave input here and there. If we share our lives together, we must be intentional in sharing work and play. On one particular weekend our family was in the mountains and my mom and I wanted to do a little bit of shopping. Michael agreed to take us out. We didn't exactly mention where we wanted to go but Michael knows us well enough to know what our first stop should be...the Jewelry Outlet. How exciting is that for him? He knew our deep desire and *allowed* us the privilege. (Michael: Amanda didn't mention that there is a discount Christian bookstore right next door that I was looking forward to shopping in!!)

Question: Do you and your husband ever have a chance to sit down and talk about just the two of you? Try to do this today. Make a special time with no other distractions and talk to your husband about his day, his plans, what he would like to do in the future, etc.

Let me take a moment here on day three to talk about in-laws. Genesis 2:24, "Therefore shall a man leave his father and his mother, and shall cleave unto his wife and they shall be one flesh." Has this been a struggle in your marriage? Our husbands should take first place in our lives under God. As much as I thought my Daddy hung the moon, when I became one with my husband, he had to take first place. Maybe it's the family gatherings and holidays with which you struggle. I suggest you always "play fair!" Find ways of being fair in visits and special meals together. Be careful that you don't fall into the trap of complaining about them. They may have some awful qualities, but try clinging to their good qualities. If you think there are none, remember, they gave you their son, the love of your life. Fortunately, I have the blessing of a terrific mother-in-love. God also blessed me with a mother who taught me the importance of being a loving and caring daughter-in-law.

Question: How long has it been since you've sent a note to your in-laws expressing to them your thankfulness and the joy you've found in their son?

Finally, as we consider the topic of communication, what about the children? How will you relate with your husband when the children are all gone? For many of you, you are just now going through this, and for others that has long past! When that time arrives when the children are no longer consuming your every minute, what will the dynamic of your relationship be? I can look at the example of my parents. They have become best friends again and do everything for each other and with each other. What a great relationship to still have! Jaynes says she believes, “the best mom of all is the one who loves her husband and gives her children the security of living within the protection of a rock-solid marriage, a marriage that exemplifies and models for them what God intended.”

We have talked about many different aspects in today’s devotional. While there is so much more that could be said on each of these topics I pray you have been refreshed and reminded of some ways that will strengthen your marriage.

The Measure of our Faithfulness - Women's Study

Daily Scripture Passage: Proverbs 4:23
*"Above all else, guard your heart,
for it is the wellspring of life."*

Thought to Consider: Safeguards for your Marriage Relationship

Quality No. 6 - Safeguards for Marriage
Homeland Security. We all as women want to feel beautiful and enjoy the compliments and attention we receive from our husbands. The Bible warns against looking elsewhere for that attention. Matthew 5:27-29 says, "You have heard that it was said to those of old, You shall not commit adultery. But I say to you that whoever looks at a woman to lust for her has already committed adultery with her in his heart. If your right eye causes you to sin, pluck it out and cast it from you; for it is more profitable for you that one of your members perish, than for your whole body to be cast into hell." That is a strong warning! If some other man has been paying you those compliments and you have the tendencies to return for more, then God's Word tells you to run in the opposite direction. "Flee from sexual immorality" (1 Corinthians 6:18). This reminds me of an Olympic runner who runs as fast as he can!. Satan is on the prowl. Read 2 Corinthians 2:11. Paul was writing to warn the mature Christians of Satan's seductive power. Jaynes says, "Abstaining from the appearance of evil is not just for appearance's sake. Most sinful behavior begins with the eyes and the mind. How have you seen this to be true? How can abstaining from the "appearance of evil" protect someone from actually doing something wrong?"

We all remember the story of David and Bathsheba (2 Samuel 11). Obviously King David did not guard his heart. Remember these ways the next time you are tempted or tested.

- David was in the wrong place at the wrong time.
- He was lonely and vulnerable.
- He knew what was right and ignored his better judgment.
- God will always provide a way of escape. (One thing I always tell my girls in youth is that God provided that escape before you got into that situation.)
- No one is above temptation.

- The Holy Spirit will convict us.

This story of David is a picture of what can happen to any of us if we are not constantly guarding our hearts. Become a mighty warrior for your marriage. Fight for it through prayer, keeping priorities right, and guarding your own heart against evil. The Proverbs 31 woman "watches over the ways of her household." Fight for your marriage with all you've got!

In closing, one of the key verses I've held onto in my marriage comes from Song of Solomon 8:7. "Many waters cannot quench love; rivers cannot wash it away." No marriage is totally safe from the ways of Satan but God has given us Biblical advice on how to safeguard it.

Sharon Jaynes gives the following ways to safeguard your marriage when it comes to other men:

- Have an accountability partner (a Christian friend) with whom you can admit any tempting thoughts. If need be, ask her to pray for you.
- Avoid contact with any man to whom you feel attracted, either emotionally or physically.
- Avoid having a male best friend.
- Avoid telling your marriage problems to another man.
- Avoid having a male confidant.
- Do not believe Satan's lies that life could be better with another man or that you've simply married the wrong person.
- Avoid being alone with another man (whether socially or professionally).
- Avoid seemingly innocent internet relationships.
- Stay connected to God through Bible study and prayer.
- Stay emotionally connected to your husband.
- Pray for your husband daily.

Often affairs occur in marriages because the relationship has "lost that loving feeling." Somewhere in life's rat race we've lost the romance. We are like the Church at Ephesus (Rev. 2:4) but God gives the church two simple steps for the Bride of Christ to renew her passion for her beloved.
#1 Remember - What drew you to your husband in the first place?
#2 Return - Revisit those places and feelings often and be creative.

If we are going to safeguard our marriages, we need to be on the offense of placing hedges of protection around ourselves that will keep us from any temptations. In the list on the previous page given by Sharon Jaynes, she offered a number of different ways to safeguard our marriages. Many of those related to the issue of flirtation. Consider for a moment, what are several ways to avoid flirting with other men or curtail them from flirting with you? Take a moment to list those.

Based on those thoughts or actions listed above by your response to the previous question, what additional steps can you take from today's list to safeguard your marriage?

Today we talked about remembering and returning in order for our passion to be renewed in our marriages. Answer the following questions and perhaps review the answers with your husband.

a. The first time I saw you I thought...

b. The thing that attracted me most about you was...

c. The first time we kissed, I felt...

d. The first time I dreamed about being married to you was...

e. The best date we ever had before we were married was…

(Material that follows returns to Michael as the writer/speaker)

ക്കരു

The Measure of our Faithfulness
Additional Resource – Raising Children

In a book by Wayne Mack entitled, "Strengthening Your Marriage" Mack addresses the issue of raising children and how this task in marriages can either draw a family together or push them apart. He notes in the book that respondents during his research gave two clear answers. Families were divided as a result of child rearing while others found unity in those same relationships. So as we continue this theme of "The Measure of our Faithfulness", I have added this brief section to stir our thoughts following some of the insights shared in his book. While we recognize that there are authorities on familial relationships, we also know that they too face challenges in raising children. So as we study, we are not placing any one of us on a pedestal of perfection in parenting. Rather, we are simply seeking to encourage one another in this God-given task.

According to Mack, the greatest point of contention among spouses begins at the most basic level – defining an agreed upon philosophy of child rearing. As believers, the opportunity for agreement on this is heightened because of our common faith. Our philosophy of child rearing should be rooted in God's Word.

As we define our philosophy of child rearing based on God's Word, we quickly discover that parenting is a joint endeavor. It is a journey that has both parents invested in the task of raising children. However, in our culture today the presence of both parents in a child's life is more and more uncommon. Homes are split by strife in the marriage relationship and children are growing up in divided lives. Still, even in the face of division and divorce, the responsibility remains on both mother and father to continue their role of being the example and guidance a child so desperately needs.

A philosophy of child rearing based in God's Word is developed using Scripture such as Exodus 20:12, where children are commanded to honor both father and mother. It continues in passages such as Proverbs 1:8, where children are instructed to "hear the instruction of your father, and do not forsake the law of your mother." This same principle is asserted again in Proverbs 6:20, "My son, keep your father's command, and do not forsake the law of your mother." So at the most basic level, a philosophy of child rearing involves both parents involved in the task of parenting and with both taking responsibility in the education and discipline of a child. It is not the task of one parent or the other. The Bible teaches a shared responsibility.

As parents seek to jointly raise their children based on a biblical philosophy of parenting, what also should be found is active leadership towards positive life choices? While raising our children in a church setting where Christ is proclaimed and Christian principles are taught certainly will go a long way in instilling biblical principles in the lives of our children, we also cannot take a passive role in the choices that our children make. Proverbs 29:15 states, "The rod and rebuke give wisdom, but a child left *to himself* brings shame to his mother." So instead of passive hope, we offer active direction. We do so by following the advice of Paul in Ephesians 6:4, "...bring them up in the training and admonition of the Lord." Training is not something that takes place in a passive setting. Ask any soldier in boot camp and they will confirm this truth. It is instead the result of discipline and direction, clearly and continually offered. If we want our children to be brought up in the Lord and to give them the best opportunities for making godly choices, we need to be active now in leading them in owning their faith and understanding our God that we love.

Active leadership in developing Christian principles within the lives of our children can certainly take place in a God-centered church setting. A great children or student ministry can certainly develop positive friendships as God's Word is clearly taught, but the assertion within the Bible is that our role as parents is greater than that of pastors or mentors. It is the parent who carries the responsibility of child rearing and training in the Lord. So as couples seek to develop a philosophy of child rearing, it must be centered on offering a clear example and clear teachings about what it means to be a follower of Christ. You may feel unprepared and inadequate for the task but know that the Lord will begin teaching you as you teach your child. He will give you the direction you need in leading your child towards godliness.

Sports are wonderful, academic achievement is important, and enjoyment of leisure time makes life fun, but when these become the center of our lives in child rearing, conflict will result. Why? Because anything that replaces God as the center of our lives has become an idol, and that cannot remain. If there is strife in your marriage right now as a result of child rearing, take a moment today to discover whether or not you are placing anything other than God at the center of your married life and your child's life. If so, it is only natural that there is conflict because God is seeking to get your attention so that you will change course and put Him back at the center of your lives.

Developing a biblically centered philosophy of child rearing will take time. In the busy-ness of our lives, we naturally gravitate towards the easiest road and the one with the least resistance. You've likely discovered in these six weeks of moving through the Ten Commandments that your children can always come up with more excuses as to why tonight is not a good night to sit down together and study the Bible. However, as you commit to simple practices like these, I believe God will begin changing the spiritual atmosphere of your family. Rather than the topic rarely discussed, faith can become the core of who you are. Rather than prayer being solely a pre-meal practice, it can become the first resource in the face of trials. That is the promise of a biblically centered philosophy of child rearing and one that will lead to a family of unity rather than division.

Even as I wrote these words of challenge based on my own reading of Wayne Mack's material, I prayed for those that would read these pages. I prayed that the message would be clear and that these thoughts would stir up a vision in your heart as to how your family might truly place Christ at the center of all that you are. I prayed that you would plug into a local church ministry where your family could identify with like-minded believers who also long to worship the Lord and grow in their faith.

The title of this book came as a result of understanding that God's laws for His children are truly the "Measure of Love". God loves us, so He commands us to refrain from certain choices that will harm us. In the same way, parenting God's way will demonstrate the "Measure of our Faithfulness" to our children, leading them to trust Christ for their every need.

Raising children is an adventure at every turn. There is seldom a day when you do not face decisions of discipline and direction. But raising children can also be a rewarding experience when there is unity between spouses on how children are to respect and respond to parenting. Pray for unity in this area and pray that God will help you to see the practical steps you need to take as parents in order to unify in a God-centered approach to raising the precious children that God has given you.

Connecting with the Commandments
WEEK SEVEN

Opening Activity: *Begin today's family time by asking your children, "What do you love for our family to do together?" For those with older children, spend some time talking about fun trips/events that you remember doing with your children while they were still younger. It may be that they will not remember all of the details that you remember from those trips.*

Purpose of Activity: Things that we do together as a family are the fun things that draw us closer to one another. But in the busy lives that we live, we often lose sight of just doing simple things together that will help us love each other and appreciate each other more.

This week's study has been about the faithfulness of husbands/wives as well as God's call to purity, and those are characteristics that build the family. In the same way, parents have the responsibility of building the unity of the family, and fun times together can help to do that.

Regardless of whether your kids are still crawling or whether they are now grown and learning how to raise their own children, you still can enhance the unity of the family by creating fun times together.

Family Discussion Time: Share together some of these thoughts…

- The hardest I've laughed with the family was when…

- The best party/Christmas that I can remember was when…

- One simple thing that stands out in my mind about our family is…

- If we could do anything better as a family, it would be…

- The biggest challenge in our family is…

Read Philippians 2:3-4 and discuss how that applies to your family:
Let nothing be done through selfish ambition or conceit, but in lowliness of mind let each esteem others better than himself. Let each of you look out not only for his own interests, but also for the interests of others.
How could you put that verse into practice this week as a family?

Pray now for your family – that you will be united together in love!

THE MEASURE OF LOVE

CHAPTER EIGHT

The Measure of our Integrity

The Measure of our Integrity

Daily Scripture Passage: Exodus 20:15-16
"You shall not steal."
"You shall not give false testimony against your neighbor."

Thought to Consider: Can People See the Effects of my Salvation?

Throughout the fall of 2010, the church where I pastor walked through a series entitled, "Faces in the Crowd". It was a series on the characters in the gospel narrative that really were background characters that were forced onto the stage as they encountered Christ. These individuals were radically changed by their encounter with Christ. As we studied these characters, we noted that if we have met Jesus, people ought to be able to tell the difference!

The Bible says that all have sinned and fall short of the glory of God. That includes you! There is nothing that you could do to earn salvation. Stop trying! But the Bible gives us good news in that the wages of sin *is* death, but the gift of God is eternal life through Christ Jesus. If we will trust in Christ as our Savior and believe in Him, we will not perish but have everlasting life. The Bible says that once we confess our sins, that God is faithful and just to forgive us our sins and to cleanse us from all unrighteousness. I pray you have already taken that step in your life. If not, please get in touch with a Christian friend, or your pastor. I want you to know what it means to have a relationship with Christ.

In response to the gift of new life that is available through Christ, we ought to be different! In John 3:8, Jesus uses the analogy of the wind. We cannot see the wind. We can only see the effects of the wind. In the same way, I cannot physically see someone being saved, but I certainly ought to be able to see the effects of that salvation. That is what we're talking about in this chapter. In that passage in John 3, Jesus was trying to help Nicodemus understand the spiritual world. Nicodemus could not get his mind out of the physical world to grasp what Jesus was saying. So Jesus used that illustration of the wind.

Can people see the effects of your salvation? How so?

We will be changing our course slightly in this chapter as we deal with two commandments in this one chapter. We will be dealing with the eighth and ninth commandment together - as the Measure of our Integrity. Our determination not to steal and not to lie is driven by the Measure of our Love for Him. Both come as a result of new life in Christ. So as we deal with this command, I want you to ask yourself the questions, "How am I demonstrating my new life in Christ by resisting stealing and lying, the focus of these two commands?"

Is there any area of your life where you might be tempted to steal, even in small ways?

What are some of the lies that you have allowed to continually show up in your life?

In the next devotional we will dive into the meaning behind these two commands.

The Measure of our Integrity

Daily Scripture Passage: Proverbs 22:1-2
*"A good name is more desirable than great riches;
to be esteemed is better than silver or gold.*

*Rich and poor have this in common:
The LORD is the Maker of them all."*

Thought to Consider: Defining the Eighth and Ninth Commands

As we began our study of the Ten Commandments I talked about how well each and every commandment applies to our lives today. I imagine that as we have traveled through the Ten Commandments you have found yourself challenged and convicted by one commandment more than another. But without a doubt, as we come to the eighth and ninth commandments, the application covers all of us. John Timmerman, in his book "Do We Still Need the Ten Commandments?," tells of some writers who have said that the purpose and scope of the eighth commandment is nothing short of armed robbery. At the other end of the spectrum are those who have said that everything that we fail to do or anything that we *should* have done constitutes robbery from our service to God, thus breaking the eighth command. The first is far too limited, but the latter would leave us handcuffed in this life. Following the second view we would live in constant fear that we might miss one of those opportunities of serving God and break God's law. We could never enjoy a moment of leisure in God's beautiful creation since enjoying leisure time would risk missing an opportunity of service to God and be in violation of God's commands. Before you cancel your vacation plans, let me say that I believe this latter view loses sight of God's grace and love. I concur with Timmerman that the right focus of the eighth commandment is, as he states, "actively seizing something that belongs to another." I believe that better depicts the intention of the eighth command. It is actively taking something that does not belong to you. Given that definition, we see how this command actually overlaps other commandments, particularly God's commandment against adultery. We are not to actively seize what belongs to someone else.

In reference to the commandment against lying or bearing false witness, Michael Horton makes several interesting observations in his book "The Law of Perfect Freedom." You may remember that in the third commandment we talked about carrying the name of the Lord. We discussed how everywhere we go we are giving a testimony of what it means to follow Christ. Horton pointed out how this ninth command is closely related to the third as this command seeks to protect *our* good name. That was a critical truth for God's people, Israel. Created in the image of God, we are to protect our name and the name of others against slander and deceit. Proverbs 22:1-2 says, "A good name is more desirable than great riches; to be esteemed is better than silver or gold. Rich and poor have this in common: The Lord is the Maker of them all!" Secondly, as God's image-bearers, we are to be people of our word. God's Word is always faithful. As His children, we are to desire the same for our own lives. Our lives should daily seek to mirror the trustworthiness of God's spoken word. Third, Horton speaks of the intrinsic value of truth. Everything that we build our lives on should be truth. I want my own life to be built on truth, not a lie. I want my ministry to reflect the true calling and passion of my heart. That's why the pulpit at our church is not just a place to come and hear messages that tickle your ears and give you a warm feeling all over. We need truth, and if that truth is sometimes painful to hear, then we must be willing to adjust our lives to the truth - not demand that the message adjust to our lives (note 2 Timothy 4:2-5). We need to hear truth because of the intrinsic value of truth in orienting our lives to Him.

We need to be a people of integrity, and that is demonstrated as we determine today to never actively seize anything that belongs to someone else, and to be people of truth at all times!

The Measure of our Integrity

Daily Scripture Passage: Luke 19:1-10 (NKJV)
"Then Jesus entered and passed through Jericho. Now behold, there was a man named Zacchaeus who was a chief tax collector, and he was rich. And he sought to see who Jesus was, but could not because of the crowd, for he was of short stature. So he ran ahead and climbed up into a sycamore tree to see Him, for He was going to pass that way. And when Jesus came to the place, He looked up and saw him, and said to him, "Zacchaeus, make haste and come down, for today I must stay at your house." So he made haste and came down, and received Him joyfully. But when they saw it, they all complained, saying, "He has gone to be a guest with a man who is a sinner."
Then Zacchaeus stood and said to the Lord, "Look, Lord, I give half of my goods to the poor; and if I have taken anything from anyone by false accusation, I restore fourfold."
And Jesus said to him, "Today salvation has come to this house, because he also is a son of Abraham; for the Son of Man has come to seek and to save that which was lost."

Thought to Consider: Paying it all Back

One of the biblical characters that is always a popular choice with children's material is Zacchaeus. Certainly if you were brought up in church, it is a story that you may have learned during your preschool years, even singing about the wee little man Zacchaeus.

Zacchaeus was a tax collector. But he was no ordinary tax collector. The Bible tells us that he was the chief tax collector. There is no doubt that he had climbed the ladder of tax collecting and now had the corner office with the view because the Bible says that he was now wealthy. But before we cast too harsh a stare at Zacchaeus, we need to be reminded that the tax collector had only one way to raise their own salary. That was accomplished by adding a percentage to the required tax of each citizen. But the temptation was too great to add a little more than a fair amount to the tax, hence the bad name for tax collectors. Apparently

Zacchaeus had done just that because following his conversion, he vows to pay back anything that he had taken wrongly.

I want to focus on the difference that took place in Zacchaeus' life when he met Jesus. All throughout Jesus' ministry there were crowds that followed him. I believe many of those in the crowd were simply fascinated with the "show". They wanted to see miracles and people angered over Jesus' words. They enjoyed the "show" but they never entered into a personal dialogue and encounter with Jesus. That was not the case for Zacchaeus. In Luke 19:3 we learn that Zacchaeus wanted to "see who Jesus was". Zacchaeus did not simply want to see what Jesus could do, but truly who he was. So he steps away from crowd. In fact, he runs out ahead of the crowd - a step that we all need to be challenged to take. After he ran out in front of the crowd, he does something completely undignified for a man of his wealth and position - he climbs a tree. (Take a look at 2 Sam. 6:12-22 for a similar story). Now climbing a tree is just fine for a kid to do, but that's no easy task for an adult - please don't try it! Zacchaeus was willing to do whatever necessary to see who Jesus was.

You have read the rest of the story. Jesus invites himself over to Zacchaeus' house and Zacchaeus has a personal encounter with his Savior that day! After Zacchaeus "welcomed him gladly" - illustrating his acceptance of Jesus - a change happens in Zacchaeus' life. He stands to his feet before Jesus and says, "Here and now I give half of my possessions to the poor, and if I have cheated anybody out of anything, I will pay back four times the amount." Zacchaeus' life had changed. In Luke 3:8 we read, "Produce fruit in keeping with repentance." That was the immediate response of Zacchaeus' new life. Having just received Jesus, he is already demonstrating the Measure of his Love for Jesus through demonstrating the Measure of his Integrity. He is producing fruit in keeping with repentance.

That puts God's eighth commandment in a whole new perspective. The desire to actively seize what belongs to someone else is no longer within me because of the fact that I have met Jesus. Now does that mean that I will no longer be tempted to sin? Absolutely not. But I will be challenged to make it right when I fall into sin. Zacchaeus demonstrated this new desire almost immediately in this huge step of faith where he desired to pay back all those that he had wronged. Did Zacchaeus wrong anyone from that point forward? He may have. But the demonstration of new life that we see at the beginning of his relationship with Christ was that he would make it right. Have you stolen? Then ask forgiveness, and now go and make it right!

The Measure of our Integrity

Daily Scripture Passage: John 4:4-19, 39-42 (NKJV)
Due to the length of today's Scripture only a portion appears printed.
"And many of the Samaritans of that city believed in Him because of the word of the woman who testified, "He told me all that I ever did." So when the Samaritans had come to Him, they urged Him to stay with them; and He stayed there two days. And many more believed because of His own word.
Then they said to the woman, "Now we believe, not because of what you said, for we ourselves have heard Him and we know that this is indeed the Christ, the Savior of the world."

Thought to Consider: A Life of Lies

The greatest joy in studying God's Word is that it is never ending in its truth and application for our lives. A story that we have known since our childhood can have new meaning as we come to God's Word in a new season of our faith. Just as we studied Zacchaeus yesterday as a familiar Bible story, today we turn our focus to the Woman at the Well.

This passage begins with the statement that Jesus "had to go through Samaria". This is a rather interesting statement because a Jew would avoid Samaria at all cost, even traveling a great distance longer just to avoid it. But this day was ordained by God. The Father willed that the Son take this journey, and Samaria was the route of the day. Now late in the day, Jesus stops at the well in hopes of getting some water to quench His thirst. There he finds a woman coming to draw water from the well. Understand that this was not the ordinary time for a woman to be coming to the well. Women would come in the morning while the day was still cool. Most have suggested that the Samaritan woman came late in the day to avoid the company of the other women and the chance for ridicule. Whatever the case, this was an appointment ordained by God. There at the well, the woman had the opportunity to learn about water she had never heard of before - the Living Water. This Living Water would quench her thirst so that she would never have to come again. While the offer of Living Water certainly intrigued the woman, it was only as the dialogue continued that she was able to truly see Jesus as Messiah. It was at the point where Jesus exposed her life of lies, and that action opened her eyes to this man at the well as Messiah.

What Jesus pointed out to the Samaritan woman that day was that she was living a lie. Her life of failed relationships had led her to the point of believing that living with the current man, who was not her husband, was the best life available to her. It is a lie that far too many believe today. But God's plan is so much greater, and that is what He wanted her to see that day. Jesus approached her not with condemnation, but with an invitation. He approached her in a way that required confession, as is always the case with Jesus. We can continue to live in a life of lies and God will allow us to reap the penalties of that lifestyle (just read about the Israelites in their journey to the Promised Land if you don't believe that). When we come before Him in confession, He will forgive our sins and cleanse us of all unrighteousness. For the woman at the well, her life of lying had been exposed through her own confession. Jesus saw her for who she really was, a future child of God, and her step of confession cleared the way for her to see Jesus for who He really was - her Savior and Messiah.

Have you allowed yourself to experience an encounter similar to the one that took place there at the well? Have you allowed Jesus to expose an area of your life where you might be living a lie? Is it in your integrity in the workplace? Is it in your relationship with your spouse? Whatever the case, He stands today ready to show Himself as Messiah as His Holy Spirit convicts our hearts. That day, the woman at the well was busy with her daily activities. But because she opened her heart to the Messiah, her life was radically changed. Did you realize that in the busyness of your day, you can have an encounter with God? You see, His Holy Spirit resides within each of us as believers. Don't wait until the consequence of sin in your own life reaps a great penalty. If you are living a life of lies in whatever aspect of your life, encounter Him today. Meet Him at the well and experience the Living Water. "We know that this man really is the Savior of the world." (Jn. 4:42)

The Measure of our Integrity

Daily Scripture Passage: Luke 6:38 (NLT)
"Give, and you will receive. Your gift will return to you in full—pressed down, shaken together to make room for more, running over, and poured into your lap. The amount you give will determine the amount you get back."

Thought to Consider: Sharing and Giving the Love of God.

Quite the opposite of a life of stealing and lying would be a life of giving and sharing truth. Let us consider today the positive application of these commands as we consider again the eighth and ninth commandments. A few chapters ago I shared about the camp experience that took place in Cheraw, SC every year for our church. There we were able to spend time with adults and young people from our church like no other time of the year. I made a lot of friends through that camp experience, including the adults who served as camp counselors. One of the interesting traditions that took place each year was the giving of a dime. That may sound strange, but we understood the importance of receiving that dime. At campfire at the end of the week we would all be given a dime by the camp pastor. We could pick one person who had become a new friend, or had meant something special to us during that week, to give our one dime (I believe we softened him up a few years later because he was even gracious enough to expand that to two dimes). There was a lot of thought that went into the giving of that dime. Often you would receive a dime from someone rather unexpectedly, and those were the ones that you cherished. There are still some of the adults today in that church who have every dime labeled and in a plaque with the year and as to who gave them that special dime.

In our materialistic society I believe we have lost the meaning behind giving. To a youth group fascinated with game systems, new clothes, and a host of other things, a dime became a prized possession because there was meaning attached to the gift. Regardless of when you are reading this material, consider the meaning attached to the gift rather than the great cost. Truly, that may be the road that you need to take so this Christmas or at an upcoming birthday for a loved one that you are not borrowing against tomorrow's day of work to finance today's purchases.

As we consider the eighth commandment, we ought to be challenged to not steal, but far above that, we should be challenged to give - and to give abundantly. We have been blessed as God's children, some more than others, and the overflow of that blessing ought to be a giving heart. Give and it will come back to you, a good measure, pressed down, shaken around, and running over (Luke 6:38)!

As we give, we are also challenged to share truth. With small children of my own, I have the opportunity each day to learn all kinds of lessons from cartoons and children's books. On the popular kid's show, "Arthur," one of the characters misunderstood this idea of sharing truth. She began telling everyone truth, even when it hurt them. I don't believe that's what God would have us do. The Bible says that our words should be "seasoned with salt" (Col. 4:6). We need to put some salt on our truth so that it tastes a little better going down. Our truth should not be in tearing down, but in building others up. And the greatest truth that we could ever share is the hope that can be found in Jesus Christ. What greater lie could we tell those around us than to give them the impression that they are alright in their current life, with no need of a Savior? We need to share the truth! We need to be bold in our witness for the Lord Jesus Christ, not because any of us are particularly good at witnessing, but because we have been commanded to do it. We must share God's truth found in Jesus Christ!

We are not to steal. Instead, we are to be giving and gracious. We are not to lie. Instead, we are to share truth and to find opportunity to share the greatest truth, Jesus Christ risen as Savior!

Connecting with the Commandments
WEEK EIGHT

Preparing for the "Connecting with the Commandments"
This week was a combined lesson of commandments 8 and 9. These were combined under the heading of "The Measure of Integrity". As you study these commandments with your children, these are certainly commandments that children wrestle with. I pray that as you study, they will understand that God's standard is integrity even as our culture regards these as the accepted norm.

Opening Illustration: In Europe there is a town called Antwerp and there in that town is a bank that has some of the most amazing diamonds in the world, and a lot of them too! Well, you can imagine that lots of people dream of having those wonderful diamonds because they are worth lots and lots of money! But some people want them so bad that they have even tried to break into the bank and steal the diamonds. In 2003, a group of men broke in the bank and then they broke into the safe that held the expensive jewelry. The safe that they broke into was one that everyone thought was impossible to break into. What did they steal? Well, those men got away with $100 million dollars worth of diamonds, jewelry, and gold. But, unlike the movies, it wasn't long before they were caught. Two weeks later they were arrested and all of them were put in prison where they still remain today!
Sometimes we watch movies and we think it is all just a game and we are excited when we see the clever crooks get away with the money or, in this case, the jewelry. But as this story proves, stealing is a bad thing. These men are now in jail, away from their families, because they made a bad choice and stole what wasn't theirs.

Application of Story: Some of you might say, "But I would never steal anything that big!" But as we study God's Ten Commandments, what we find in the Bible is that we are not to steal *anything*, regardless of its value. So in God's eyes, if we steal someone's pencil or we steal someone's coins out of their desk...that's the same thing as stealing lots and lots of things like those men in Europe did. Stealing is stealing, no matter how much it is worth.

When we say we believe in and love God, He wants us to be different. He wants us to be honest. He wants us to tell the truth. We are to be different because when people look at us, they should see what God is like. If we are honest, that helps people to understand that God is honest. If we never steal,

then people will see that loving God leads you to make good choices. So stealing is always something we have to avoid!

But this week, we have also studied about telling the truth. God says in the Ten Commandments that we are not to bear false witness against our neighbor. That's just another way of saying, "Don't lie to one another."

A Lie and the Truth: Have your kids tell one true story about someone or something that happened at school and then have them tell you one that they have made up. Try to convey the idea that they are to do their best to not make the false story obvious. After they tell both stories, your job is to figure out which story is make believe and which story is true.
Follow Up: That activity was a fun way to help us see how sometimes it's hard to know whether a story is true or false. That's why God commands us to always tell the truth. It's okay to have fun with people as you make jokes and laugh together, but lying is never to be a daily habit of a believer. God wants us to tell the truth all of the time.

Proverbs 12:22 says, "Lying lips are an abomination to the Lord, but those who deal truthfully are His delight."
The words "an abomination to the Lord" means this is something that God detests or hates. Those are strong words. God actually hates it when we lie. But take a look at the rest of the verse. It basically says, "but God loves people who tell the truth."
Sibling Fights: Sometimes we know when we are doing things that make each other mad, especially for those of you with brothers or sisters. There are times when you do things that you know will make your brother or sister mad.
But there in Prov. 12, the Bible is telling us not only what will make God mad...but it also tells us what will make God glad! We need to be careful to never do those things that we know will disappoint God and to always do those things that God loves!
Application of Today's Lesson: Let's make a real effort this week to do what God loves by telling the truth. Rather than tell lies about a story or about someone, let's try our very best this week to tell the truth. Because this is something God loves, God will help you to tell the truth this week.
And just as God will help you tell the truth, He will also help you to avoid the temptations to take what is not yours by stealing. So let's pray that God will help all of us live in such a way that people will really be able to see that we love God and want to live for Him!
Close in a family prayer time.

THE MEASURE OF LOVE

CHAPTER NINE

The Measure of our Satisfaction

Introduction to Final Week

What a terrific journey this has been! In each chapter we have had the opportunity to study God's Ten Commandments on a daily basis and to seek to apply those to our lives. We have faced the reality that each of God's commandments has unique relevance to our lives today, and that we all stand guilty of breaking His commands. But praise be unto God for his wonderful grace demonstrated through Jesus Christ where we discover forgiveness and mercy in our time of need. The Ten Commandments reveal our need for a Savior. In the Ten Commandments, we discover that we are sinners, but while we were still sinners, Christ died for us. That is the wonderful truth that brings hope to our study of these commands. God's commands are the Measure of His Love for us as precepts by which to live. But the greatest Measure of His Love for us is demonstrated in Him sending His one and only Son to die on the cross to pay the penalty for his rebellious children. I pray that this study has done nothing less than draw you unto God in worship and praise for His indescribable mercy and grace. May the Measure of our Love be demonstrated by our desire to be obedient to His commands!

ବ୍ଧ

The Measure of our Satisfaction

Daily Scripture Passage: Exodus 20:17
"You shall not covet your neighbor's house. You shall not covet your neighbor's wife, or his manservant or maidservant, his ox or donkey, or anything that belongs to your neighbor."

Hebrews 13:5
"Keep your lives free from the love of money and be content with what you have, because God has said,
"Never will I leave you;
never will I forsake you."

Thought to Consider: Living in Freedom

All the kids in the neighborhood were talking about them. It was the coolest thing on the market. You could do bunny-hops, rail slides, ramp jumps, and a host of other things that make no sense to most of you. Whatever it had the capability of doing, I had to have one. So I began the hinting, begging, and the pleading for a scooter. But not just any old scooter, I had to have the Mongoose® Scooter. Why a Mongoose®? Well the reason is clear. The Mongoose® Scooter had handlebars that could turn a full 360 degrees without the brake cables getting twisted like some of the other ones. Not that I knew how to make it do that, but I just had to have the one that could! The begging, the pleading, and the constant hints must have been successful that year because that Christmas I received a shiny, new, orange Mongoose® Scooter! I was the subject of awe as I strolled through the neighborhood that Christmas morning. No doubt children were glued to their windows in envy of my new scooter. I imagine the shiny white tires and fresh paint were sparkling in the cold winter sun on that Christmas day. Life was wonderful!

But I learned a fascinating truth about scooters in the days that followed. You may be noticing in the picture that these things don't have pedals. Not only did it not have pedals, but it did not have a motor either. No, all it had were two wheels and a platform. Now that might be just fine if you lived in a flat coastal town, but my community was nothing but hills and valleys, and our home sat in the lowest valley! Sure this fancy new scooter was pretty, but I discovered a more important fact - it was exhausting! On top of that, it never

did *any* of those tricks they advertised! Every time I tried any of those fancy tricks, I got wrapped up in those very brake cables that were suppose to be designed for the ultimate of tricks! The harsh reality of my incredible scooter turned out to be far from the dreams I had envisioned.

Is that not true for so many things in our lives? The image and the anticipated pleasure is so grand that we create an unrealistic expected result. We believe that acquiring that dream item will certainly be the source of our future happiness. But how often has that proven to be true?

In this chapter we are talking about the final commandment of the Ten Commandments - "Do not covet your neighbor's house. You shall not covet your neighbor's wife, or his manservant, or his maidservant, his ox or donkey, or anything that belongs to your neighbor."

At the root of coveting is greed. Greed is defined as "a selfish and excessive desire for more of something than is needed." You might say, "I am not a greedy person." In a sense, that might be true. But do you ever desire more of something than you really need? I dare say that most of us at one time or another have done so. As a society, we are overrun with the sin of coveting.

While our modern day terminology reduces coveting to " wishing for earnestly," it is so much more than that. Coveting is "not only to have an inordinate desire for something but to take steps to get the desired thing."[1] It is an "insatiable desire for more and more - beyond any human need."[2] The command not to covet does not, as Jerry Vines says, require a "cessation of desire." Being commanded to not covet does not mean that we are to no longer desire anything. We can still desire a better education, to improve our position at work, or to better our living conditions. But these cannot become an "insatiable desire for more and more." This cannot become the consuming passion of our lives to the extent that we are no longer seeking first the kingdom and His righteousness. I believe we can best understand coveting when we understand the ultimate motivation of our desires. Is the focus of my desire such that I am still seeking God's kingdom or am I now seeking my own? Our focus should never be on the building of our own kingdom.

As we begin our study in this chapter of the tenth commandment, spend some time considering how this commandment applies to your own life. Consider how coveting has caused you to make irrational purchases and/or decisions. Begin today to seek God's will and plan for how this chapter of study can affect your daily walk with Christ.

The Measure of our Satisfaction

Daily Scripture Passage: Philippians 3:7-8
"But whatever was to my profit I now consider loss for the sake of Christ. What is more, I consider everything a loss compared to the surpassing greatness of knowing Christ Jesus my Lord, for whose sake I have lost all things. I consider them rubbish, that I may gain Christ."

Thought to Consider: Becoming Dissatisfied with Things

I was driving to the office on the day of this devotional and knew that God had given me this image to illustrate the point for this chapter. As I passed one of the homes on our road, I noticed the farmer's cattle all crowded near the fence. The cows were grazing and living what I imagine is the exciting life of a cow. But I noticed one cow in particular. This cow was not content with the acres and acres of grass throughout the field. No, this cow only wanted the grass on the other side of the fence. Understand, in order to get to this grass on the other side of the fence, it had to weave its head through the barbed wire fence and hold its head low to the ground just to stay below the fencing. But that was no problem, because I am confident that this grass on the other side of the fence was a delicacy worth the pain and discomfort!

In our passage, Paul makes a strong declaration against his former life. As a Pharisee, Paul was resolutely determined to be the Pharisee of Pharisees. In the previous verses he says, "If anyone thinks he has reasons to put confidence in the flesh, I have more." One might say that Paul had climbed the ladder of Pharisaical righteousness, and no doubt this assent was difficult. With 613 laws, can you imagine the pop quizzes? Paul had dedicated his life to the law. Then that all changed. His perspective was radically altered by an encounter with the Lord Jesus Christ. From that point forward we see the new focus and perspective of Paul, scoffing at his former life and exalting Christ alone. As John MacArthur says, "All of the cherished treasures in his gain column suddenly became deficits." They meant nothing in comparison to Christ. It was a radical shift in priority.

Paul continues to describe his former way of life, even using the imagery of rubbish or trash. The word rubbish used here literally means "dung," "manure," or "waste". What a change in perspective! A short time before these religious credits would have been the trophies lining his walls. Now

they are nothing more than smelly trash headed for the landfill. Why? Because it was rubbish in comparison to knowing Christ more. Anything that threatened to interfere with him knowing Christ more was rubbish in need of being discarded. Paul considered them all rubbish that he might gain Christ.

Are the material things and possessions of this world consuming your focus and deterring you from knowing Christ more? Many of us would have to say yes to that question because our work, bills, and wants capture our attention more than our thoughts of Christ. We pass it off as just "the way life is". You *have* to work and you *have* to pay the bills. There's just no way around it. This is true. We *do* have to provide for our families and perform to the top of our abilities at work. But I do not believe that conforming to the truth of the tenth commandment excludes either of those. The question is this: Do all these things seem as loss in comparison to knowing Christ? Do they all seem totally insignificant in comparison to growing closer to the God who loves you so? I imagine that we all need to step back and take a look at our 21st century lives and say, "Have we really figured out what life is really all about?"

Count it all as rubbish in comparison to knowing Christ. The things of this world will pass away, but the relationship with Christ you build on today will reap rewards in this life and beyond. Spend time in prayer right now. Ask God to help you think on Him. Stay in prayer until the worries of work or school begin to fade away as you focus on the surpassing greatness of Christ!

ക്ക

The Measure of our Satisfaction

Daily Scripture Passage: 1 Timothy 6:6-11
[6] *Now godliness with contentment is great gain.* [7] *For we brought nothing*
into this world, and it is certain[a] *we can carry nothing out.* [8] *And having*
food and clothing, with these we shall be content. [9] *But those who desire*
to be rich fall into temptation and a snare, and into many foolish and
harmful lusts which drown men in destruction and perdition. [10] *For the*
love of money is a root of all kinds of evil, for which some have strayed
from the faith in their greediness, and pierced themselves through with
many sorrows.
[11] *But you, O man of God, flee these things and pursue righteousness,*
godliness, faith, love, patience, gentleness.

Thought to Consider: Wrestling with Contentment

Mention the word "wrestling" and all kinds of images come to mind. Flashing lights, cameras, high drama, and a host of other things fill your mind. That type of wrestling is not what I am going to talk about. What I am considering is high school, college, and Olympic wrestling. Those are quite different than the soap opera of television wrestling. One of the keys to wrestling competitively is training. My middle brother and I both wrestled. Well, let me clarify, he did well at wrestling and I warmed the bench for a couple of years. But when it came to practice time, everyone was equal. Everyone had to do the sprints, push-ups, crunches, and exercises regardless of whether you started or not. While I despised the endless practices in the midst of them, I appreciated them when it came time to wrestle. Our team was consistently in better shape than our competition because of the conditioning that took place throughout the week. Our coach knew that preparation was key to success.

When we consider the issue of coveting, we need to do some preparation. A part of that preparation is realizing the empty promises that coveting offers. That's what we're looking at today. Allow this material to be your training for this chapter. If you prepare yourself now, you will be better equippped when you face a time of temptation.

John Piper spends a great deal of time dealing with these false promises in his book, *Future Grace*. As we continue today, I want to highlight the five false promises that Piper highlights and comment on each briefly.

The first empty promise of coveting is this:
Covetousness never brings satisfaction.

Ecclesiastes 5:10 says, "He who loves money will not be satisfied with money; nor he who loves abundance with its income: this is also vanity." Money is certainly necessary for life. But the problem comes in fascination with money, which is such an easy road to take. This fascination can overtake those with or those without money.
You have probably seen this principle played out within your own life. If you are a computer user, you have witnessed this in software sales again and again. At the time of the writing of this material, Microsoft was scheduled to come out with their new operating platform called "Microsoft Vista." It replaced WindowsXP as the current operation system of Microsoft. In anticipation of this new platform, the marketing touted the mediocrity of XP in comparison to Vista. Since then, Windows 7 has become the standard. There is a continual marketing plan for coveting. Coveting never brings satisfaction because there will always be a "better one" about to come out!

Covetousness chokes off spiritual life.
The worries of this world can choke out your spiritual life. When the focus of my eyes and my heart turn away from God, the life of my walk with God will be choked out. The desire of our heart should be to honor God above all else and to glorify Him with our lives. But doing this becomes very difficult when coveting has dug a financial hole or caused a break in relationships from which there is a long road of recovery. Coveting can choke out your spiritual life.

Covetousness spawns many other sins.
1 Timothy 6:10 says, "The love of money is the root of all evils." Many of you have experienced this first hand, so you need little explanation. Others of you are going through the truth of this verse right now. But while some of us have learned this lesson, there are others who are blinded by this truth. I pray that today you will begin to address the sin of coveting - of desiring what another has and seeking that "thing" at whatever cost. That road will be filled with bumps, detours, and a host of other sins will result. That's why God commands us to flee from it. If

you can't help but covet something in that new catalog, cancel the catalog. Remove the temptation from in front of your eyes before it leads to sin. Covetousness spawns many other sins.

Covetousness lets you down when you need help most.

Bill Cosby used to say, "I brought you into this world, and I can take you out." It's a line that has been repeated by many parents seeking to instill a bit of comical fear into their children. The Bible speaks in similar terms in 1 Timothy 6:7 where we read, "You brought nothing into this world, and you're taking nothing out" (my paraphrase of course).

A fisherman was laid back on the deck of his boat when another fisherman came by. The man said, "Why aren't you out there fishing?" The resting man said, "Because I've caught enough fish for today." Well that just didn't make sense to this industrious man. He said, "Why don't you catch more fish than you need?" To this the resting man replied, "What would I do with them?" That's a great question the industrious man thought. He said, "You could earn more money and buy a better boat so that you could go deeper and catch more fish. You could purchase nylon nets, catch even more fish, and make more money. Soon you'd have a fleet of boats and be rich like me." The fisherman asked, "Then what would I do?" To which the industrious fisherman replied, "You could sit down and enjoy life."[1] Coveting baits you with a lie and delivers an empty result.

In the end covetousness destroys the soul.

1 Timothy 6:9 says, "Those who desire to be rich fall into temptation, into a snare, into many senseless and hurtful desires that plunge men into ruin and destruction."

We'll be talking about this more in the final devotional, but realize that coveting can ruin your marriage, your intimate relationship with Christ, your integrity, and so many areas of your life. It is truly a commandment with far-reaching consequences.

Until we become dissatisfied and disgusted with our coveting nature, we will never conquer this sin. We need to be bold enough to recognize the sin in our lives and take deliberate steps away from that sin. I pray that today's devotional has helped to open our eyes to the empty promises of coveting. Find contentment in Christ alone. "But whatever was to my profit I now consider loss for the sake of Christ" (Philippians 3:7).

The Measure of our Satisfaction

Daily Scripture Passage: 2 Corinthians 4:18
"while we do not look at the things which are seen, but at the things which are not seen. For the things which are seen *are* temporary, but the things which are not seen *are* eternal."

Thought to Consider: Finding Satisfaction in Christ Alone

Myopia is "a condition in which the visual images come to a focus in front of the retina of the eye resulting especially in defective vision of distant objects." We know it best as nearsightedness. You are able to see items close up, but items at a distance are blurred. Now I am no eye doctor and I would probably fail miserably at identifying the different parts of the eyball, so I am going to leave the eye condition diagnoses to the ophthalmologists. But I am going to make a spiritual diagnosis. What I believe is true of us today is that far too many of us are suffering from spiritual myopia.

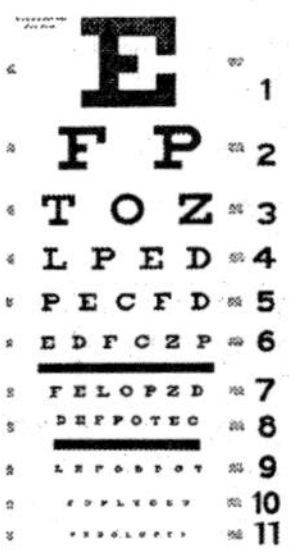

The remedy for this condition is finding our satisfaction in Christ alone. As John Piper says in his book *Future Grace*, "covetousness is desiring something so much that you lose your contentment in God. The opposite of covetousness is contentment in God. When contentment in God decreases, covetousness for gain increases." The goal of my Christian faith ought to be daily becoming more and more like Christ. The best way to illustrate this is to daily demonstrate my contentment in Him. I am content in His instructions, so I obey them. I am content in His precepts, so I study them. I ought to long for contentment in Christ alone.

But we discover in Scripture that contentment is not automatic. You have probably discovered that by now in your own Christian life. In Philippians 4:11-12 we read, "Not that I speak in regard to need, for *I have learned* in whatever state I am, to be content: I know how to be abased, and I know how to abound. Everywhere and in all things I have learned both to be full and to be hungry, both to abound and to suffer need" (italics mine). We can learn from studying Philippians that this was a church that had long supported Paul, both in their prayers and finances. He wanted to thank them for their gift, but also to communicate that this was not his only reason for his love for this church. The help that Epaphroditus brought from the church was greatly appreciated, but not in greed or covetousness. Paul had *learned* what it meant to be content. Contentment is not automatic! It must be learned.

I believe this is a task that is beyond our ability to "buckle-down" and pull off in our strength. Rather, we claim the words of Philippians 4:13, "I can do all things through Him who gives me strength." I must trust that I can accomplish this task only through God's strength. Following that, I will rest in the promise of vs. 19 which says, "And my God will meet all your needs according to his glorious riches in Christ Jesus." He will provide for ALL my needs.

In my own life there is a glaring difference between all my *needs* and all my *wants*. What Paul is referring to in this passage is, as John Piper says, "all that you need for God-glorifying contentment." In my own strength I cannot turn my eyes away from the lure of every new thing or that which I do not have. But I *can* do all things through Christ who strengthens me. And within that, I can begin to find total contentment in God supplying my every need so that I experience God-glorifying contentment.

Help us Lord to focus our eyes not just on what is right before us, but to fix our eyes on what is unseen, and to grow our faith in Your provision, not our own. Help us to discover God-glorifying contentment and to experience new freedom in our faith and trust in God!

The Measure of our Satisfaction

Daily Scripture Passage: Luke 12:15-21
"Then he said to them, "Watch out! Be on your guard against all kinds of greed; a man's life does not consist in the abundance of his possessions." And he told them this parable: "The ground of a certain rich man produced a good crop. He thought to himself, 'What shall I do? I have no place to store my crops.'
"Then he said, 'This is what I'll do. I will tear down my barns and build bigger ones, and there I will store all my grain and my goods. And I'll say to myself, "You have plenty of good things laid up for many years. Take life easy; eat, drink and be merry." '
"But God said to him, 'You fool! This very night your life will be demanded from you. Then who will get what you have prepared for yourself?'
"This is how it will be with anyone who stores up things for himself but is not rich toward God."

Thought to Consider: A Commandment with Far-Reaching Consequences

The first and tenth commandments have often been called the bookends for the Ten Commandments, and fittingly so. At the beginning of this study of the Ten Commandments we talked about how the first command, "no other gods before me," shows itself in many of the other commands. Now, as we finish our study of the Ten Commandments, we can see how this final command has application in many of the other commands much the same. Not coveting will keep us from making an idol of things before God. Not coveting will keep us from working on through a day of rest as God designed it. Coveting can result in murder, demonstrated by a recent case where a teen killed another teen for one reason - to take his shoes. So not coveting can prevent murder. The tenth command includes coveting your neighbor's wife, so not coveting can protect us from adultery. Not coveting can keep us from stealing or lying. It is a commandment with far-reaching consequences because it addresses multiple commands.

Today's passage is an interesting story. A man received an abundance of crops in a particular year. It was an incredible blessing. The crop was so large that the man had no where to store all of the food. Being a practical man, he realized that he needed bigger barns. So he brought down the inadequate barns and replaced them with barns appropriate for the big crop he had reaped. What an idea! Now he had the option of kicking back, taking it easy for a while. He had worked hard for those crops, and now he had an overflow. We would call that good planning and a healthy return on his investment. We would applaud his hard work and thoughtful planning, and we would apparently be right in doing so. But this story is not about economics and business. If that were the case, then this man would have been honored for his decisions. No, this is a story about the motivation of this man's heart. To understand the perspective of the story, just read vs. 21. There we read, "This is how it will be with anyone who stores up things for himself but is not rich toward God." The man had discovered that he was rich, so much so that he was planning to retire. But his heart never turned toward God. He made an idol of his abundance, placing it before God. He was covetous and greedy because we do not see him considering how he might help those around him whose crops might have been less productive. He was rich in things, but he was poor in God.

I believe what we need to see in our passage for today is that we must be challenged to realize of what our life now consists. It is not in the abundance of possessions, but *in Christ*. Does that mean that God's people can't have abundance? I certainly do not think that is the case. However, the abundance of possessions can serve to be a great distraction from where true life is found - in Christ. Fortunately, I have personally witnessed individuals who have been incredibly blessed in this life and yet their focus remains on Christ. They give of their possessions freely as the Lord leads them. But this man's great abundance turned his eyes onto what he was able to store up. He was suffering from spiritual myopia!

Realize today that this is a commandment with far-reaching consequences. This man probably never realized the greed and covetousness of his own heart until he experienced great abundance. You may be seeing hints of that even within yourself as you have read this chapter, whether it is the result of abundance or a great lack of. In either case, are you suffering from spiritual myopia? Find satisfaction in Christ alone. Experience the joy of trusting Him each and every day!

Connecting with the Commandments
WEEK NINE

Preparing for the Connecting Time: *As I wrote each of these "Connecting with the Commandments" lessons, I thought about how God often teaches me so much as I study His Word...but often my kids do not have the opportunity to share in that lesson learned. So rather than just make this a study for adults as it was in the first printing, I decided to add these family time lessons. Hopefully you have been able to adapt these to your kids and your family so that you have enjoyed spending time together in God's Word. Each of these lessons were tried out on our own kids and tweaked as they responded or lost interest - so these were "kid tested and parent approved"! We look forward to hearing from you how these lessons impacted your family.*

In our final lesson on the Ten Commandments, today we look at God's command to be content with what He has given us. The last commandment said that we are not to covet our neighbor's house or a list of other things. To covet means we think what someone else has is better than what we have and that leads us to want it really, really bad. In fact, the idea here is that we want it so bad that we'll do anything to get it. That kind of strong desire is a bad thing because God wants us to be happy with what we have. Sure it is okay to want really nice things, but we can't always be looking around us at what others have and wishing we had those things. Those thoughts can lead us to not like people around us just because they have more than us. Instead, we are to be grateful for what God has given us and not judge others by the things they have.

Toy Ads: Do you remember all of the Christmas advertisements for all of the latest toys this past year? There were some really good toys this past year and there are always toys each year that become the hot item. But sometimes those really famous toys can end up not being so great. In fact, according to one article, Fisher-Price had to recall 11 million toys in just one year because the toys ended up being dangerous. So something that at one time was the toy everyone wanted can sometimes end up being the toy everyone wanted to send back to the company!
That fact reminds us that keeping our eyes on things all of the time is a bad thing. The very stuff that we once wanted so badly can end up being no good at all. But if we are grateful for what we already have, well that's a good thing. Instead of always wanting more, we just enjoy what we have been

given. That's called contentment - a big word for saying you are happy with what you already have. God wants us to keep our focus on Him and loving Him more, not things.

Think about it...what did you get as a Christmas or Birthday gift last year? What about two years ago? You might be able to remember the big, long awaited gift, but many times we get lots of gifts and the memory of those toys quickly fade away as they end up at the bottom of the toy box.

So what God is challenging us to remember is to always be content with what He gives us. That's not just about toys and things, it's also in how He gives us abilities and talents that we can use for Him! If God made you a singer, then sing for God. If God made you an artist, then draw beautiful pictures that tell people God's story. If God made you a great runner or athlete, then give God the credit when you win! Rather than always wish that God had made you someone else, thank God today for the way that He made you - totally unique and His perfect design!

Prayer Time: As you close today's family time, pray together as a family that God would help all of you to put HIM at the center of everything that you do. Ask God to help you to be content with the things He has given you and the ways He has designed you as a special creation. Ask God to help you not to always want what others have, but to be happy with what you have already!

෴

Conclusion

You now have the evidence and have studied this case thoroughly. You have wrestled with the material and asked some difficult questions of yourself. You have now invested a great deal of time in studying God's Ten Commandments. It is now time for the verdict. I hope that you have come to the same verdict as I have - the Ten Commandments are without a doubt the Measure of God's Love for His children. They are precepts and loving commands from a God who desires us to live a life that brings glory to Him. I pray that your perspective on the Ten Commandments has radically changed over these chapters in a way that you now see their great application and relevance to your life today. Very early on in my study of these commandments I realized that if we were to get a grasp on living out these Ten Commandments in our lives each and every day, our lives as believers would be radically different. While we will never fully conquer sin in this lifetime, I believe that as we seek to live out these commandments through God's strength, that we will experience a new level of maturity in our faith and victory over these sins.

God spoke these commandments because He knows us intimately. As I have said many times throughout this study, these are not restrictions from a harsh dictator, but the Measure of His Love for us so that we might live that abundant life that He gives us. He knows that we are tempted to place other things before Him. He knows that we make an idol of all too many things within our lives. He knows that we fail to rightly carry His name. He knows that we need rest. He sees the great need for honoring father and mother. He knows that our heart can be filled with hatred, even murder. He knows that our wandering eyes and lack of boundaries in our relationships can lead to harmful choices, even adultery. He knows that our coveting natures will lead us down a dark road, even stealing or living a lie. No, these are not harsh rules from a dictator, but loving commands prescribed by our Heavenly Father.

I was reading an article on a friend's website that challenged me in my walk and ministry. He talked about learning more and more about God. He talked about how learning ought to challenge us to love God more and to seek to live for Him. As I considered that challenge, I boiled it all down to just these three words: Learn, Love, Live. The more that I learn about God, the more that I love Him, and the more I will want to live for Him. It's really that simple. Our study of these Ten Commandments has taught us a great deal about the love of God. It has taught us a great deal about the great difference that ought to exist between the life of a believer and a non-believer. But more than anything else, it should challenge us to do just those three things: Learn, Love, Live.

I am praying for you as you continue this incredible journey of faith. Go learn. Go love. Go live.

Selection of Resource Materials

Bill Bright, *Written by the Hand of God* (Orlando, Florida: NewLife Publications, 2001).

Joshua Harris, *Not Even a Hint* (Sisters, Oregon: Multnomah, 2003).

Michael S. Horton, *The Law of Perfect Freedom* (Chicago: Moody Press, 1993).

Bill Hybels, *Engraved on Your Heart* (Colorado Springs, Colorado: Victor Press, 1985, 2000).

Jerry B. Jenkins, *Loving Your Marriage Enough to Protect It* (Chicago: Moody Press, 1989, 1993).

D. James Kennedy, *Why the Ten Commandments Matter* (New York: Warner Faith, 2005).

John MacArthur, *Philippians: John MacArthur New Testament Commentary* (Chicago, Moody Press, 2001).

Ron Mehl, *The Tender Commandments* (Sisters, Oregon: Multnomah, 1998).

John Piper, *Future Grace* (Sisters, Oregon: InterVarsity Press, 1995).

Ibid., *Holy, Holy, Holy is the Lord of Hosts* (Desiring God Ministries: http://www.desiringgod.org).

Ernest C. Reisinger, *Whatever Happened to the Ten Commandments?* (Carlisle, Pennsylvania, 1999).

Fred Stoeker and Stephen Arterburn, *Every Man's Battle* (Colorado Springs, Colorado: WaterBrook Press, 2000).

John H. Timmerman, *Do we still need the Ten Commandments?* (Minneapolis: Augsburg Fortress, 1997).

LaVergne, TN USA
30 March 2011
222235LV00001B/19/P